# A ROUND OF SCOTTISH COURSES

Back Nine Press
Chicago, Illinois
www.back9press.com
@backninepress



9 8 7 6 5 4 3 2 1

First Edition
Printed in the United States of America.

Library of Congress Cataloging-in-Publication Data: 2026930814
Hartsell, Jim.
A Round of Scottish Courses
By Jim Hartsell
Back Nine Press (USA)
pages cm

ISBN 978-1-956237-42-9 (hardback)
ISBN 978-1-956237-43-6 (e-book)

# A ROUND OF SCOTTISH COURSES

## JIM HARTSELL

Foreword by Lorne Rubenstein
Afterword by Stephen Proctor

BACK NINE PRESS

*For David MacBrayne of Campbeltown
and Greg McCrae of Brodick*

# CONTENTS


Foreword by Lorne Rubenstein ............. ix

Introduction ............................. 1


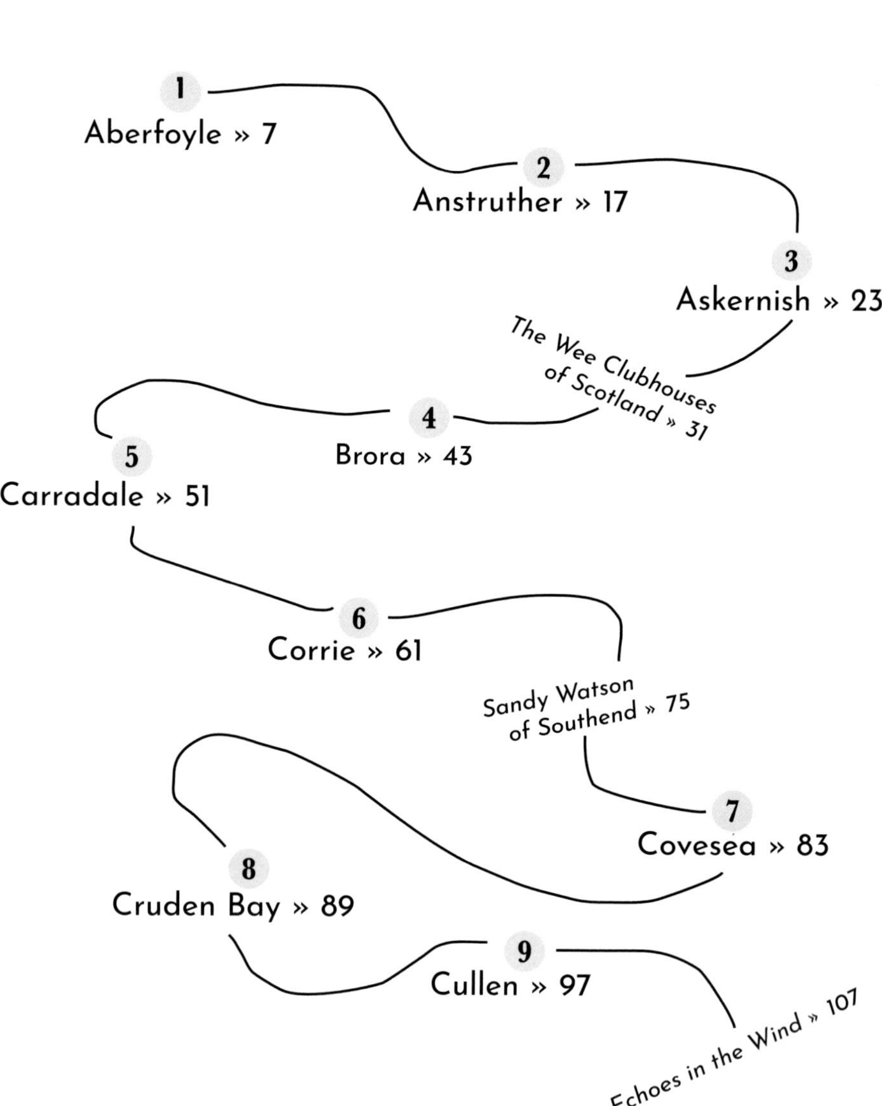


**1** Aberfoyle » 7

**2** Anstruther » 17

**3** Askernish » 23

The Wee Clubhouses of Scotland » 31

**4** Brora » 43

**5** Carradale » 51

**6** Corrie » 61

Sandy Watson of Southend » 75

**7** Covesea » 83

**8** Cruden Bay » 89

**9** Cullen » 97

Echoes in the Wind » 107

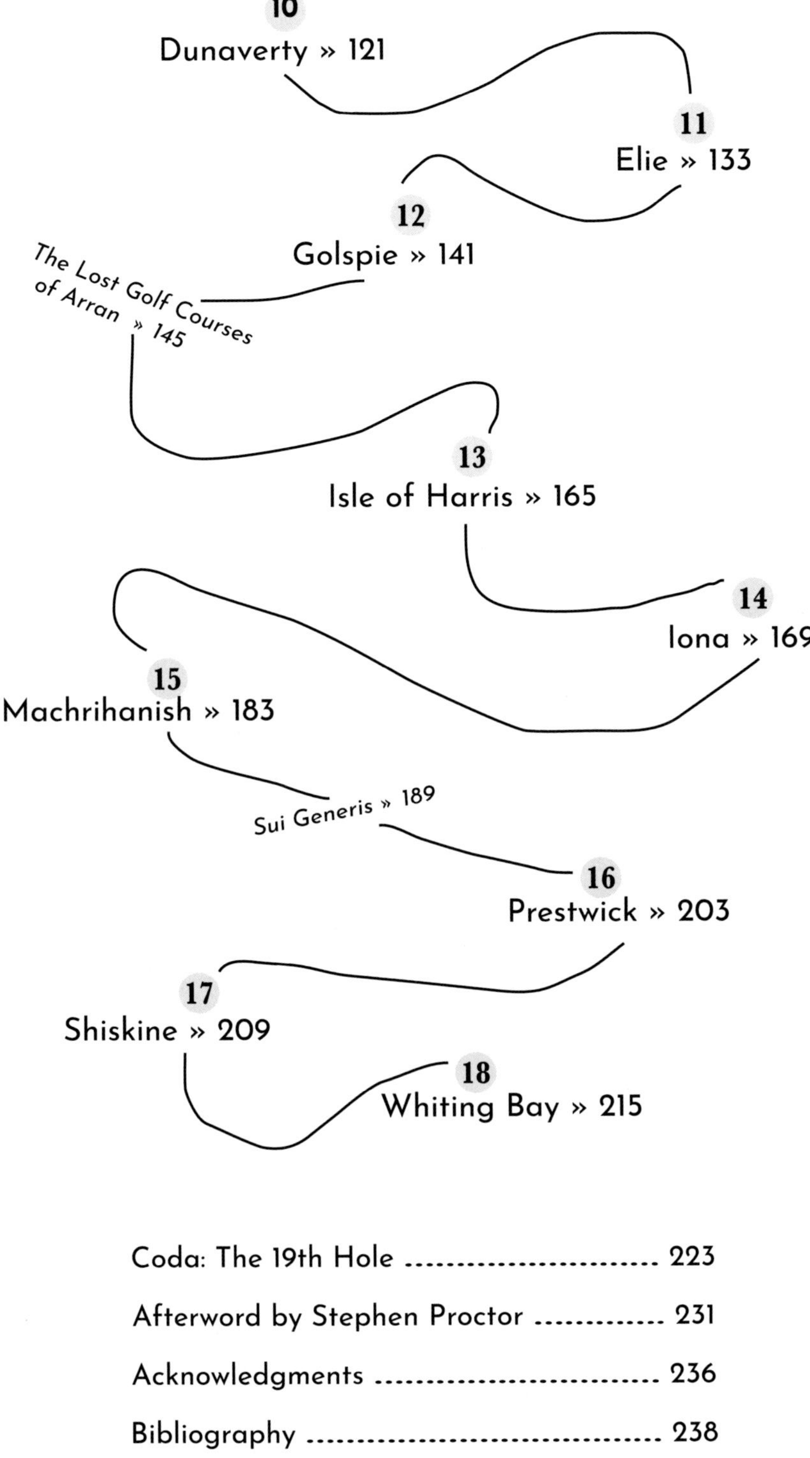


**10** Dunaverty » 121

**11** Elie » 133

**12** Golspie » 141

The Lost Golf Courses of Arran » 145

**13** Isle of Harris » 165

**14** Iona » 169

**15** Machrihanish » 183

Sui Generis » 189

**16** Prestwick » 203

**17** Shiskine » 209

**18** Whiting Bay » 215

Coda: The 19th Hole .......................... 223

Afterword by Stephen Proctor .............. 231

Acknowledgments ............................ 236

Bibliography ................................. 238

THE GOLF COURSE, BLACKWATERFOOT, ISLE OF ARRAN
B 2371

# FOREWORD

## BY LORNE RUBENSTEIN

To travel fully in the world of golf is not only to play courses, although that is part of the experience. It is not only to meet fellow travelers and locals and to enjoy their company on the course and at 19th holes over a drink, while telling stories and making new friends. It is not only to learn about the area in which one is traveling, thereby enriching one's adventure. It is all this and more, but more than anything, at least in my experience, it is the letting oneself become absorbed in and by the brew, the cocktail, the heady mixture that simply "being" somewhere new produces.

Jim Hartsell is open to every moment, person, golf hole, and vista he encounters during what I can only describe as his "ramble" through the multi-varied golf life that Scotland offers. It is there in the links and the towns where golf is everyday recreation, where one encounters what can be called "simple" golf. To me, that is the highest compliment to the beating heart of Scottish golf, and to the pulse that crackles throughout Jim's narrative. I have made perhaps 30 visits to Scotland over the years, to play the ancient game and to cover Open championships, and to spend a summer at the Royal Dornoch Golf Club and to live in the town. I have traveled widely and eagerly throughout Scotland, and thought I have been everywhere. But I haven't. I hadn't. Now, however, Jim's explorations, his open-mindedness and the deep pleasure he takes in "being" in the country, have awakened me to so much I hadn't seen.

The reader will find expressions in this book of something unique to Scottish golf, and the more rugged it is, the quirkier it is, the better, enriching, and more fulfilling it is. Jim finds that he frequently gains energy after a day's golf, and that day might include 36 or 45 holes. How is it possible that one will feel stronger and hardier after a full day of walking a links? Shouldn't a day spent walking perhaps 10 miles tire one out? But the opposite happens to Jim and his companions, which often include his son Jake. Scottish golf refreshes and revitalizes him, even after travel that can be exhausting. There is something in the air in Scottish golf.

Jim's account of the valuable time he has spent during 15 visits to Scotland over the years, and while playing so many of what he calls "the small, hidden courses," is an account of falling in love and being in love. Does that sound sentimental and romantic? So be it. Jim's writing has spirit. He brings the eye of an architect to what he observes in the links of Scotland—he is, after all, a professional architect. He infuses his descriptions of courses such as Isle of Harris in the Outer Hebrides, the Dunaverty Golf Club—his Scottish home of golf, "the links my soul loves best," he writes, and sweet 12-hole Shiskine Golf and Tennis Club, with the language and rhythm of a poet. Jim's writing swings.

And oh, the people he meets: this one is an artist, whose paintings I enjoyed on his website; this one knows everything about cows; this one will take you to a ceilidh, where you will enjoy traditional Gaelic folk music; this one will educate you about the true story of the film *Whisky Galore*. You are in for something special as you read this treasure. Jim writes of encountering a grandfather with two small children at the nine-hole Bute Golf Club, and watching them play a couple of holes. I was reminded of seeing four generations playing the Braid Hills course in Edinburgh some 35 years ago—a couple of kids, their father, grandfather, and great-grandfather. He writes of learning about the lost courses of the Isle of Arran by being invited to view a collection of historical postcards from the 1890s to the 1950s. The late gentleman Stuart Gough, "an obsessive collector," had assembled these. His wife Heather had invited Jim to view the collection. One thing leads to another for the traveler open to whatever the day might bring.

Page after page here transported me to what Hartsell calls the "tiny chapels of golf," with stops at renowned links such as the Old Course, Machrihanish, and Prestwick. If you've not been to Scotland, you will want to go after reading about Hartsell's round of Scottish courses. If you've been there, you will want to go again, and soon.

SOUTHEND, KINTYRE FROM EAST.
B.3547

# INTRODUCTION

"Here is superb natural golfing land, on the links of Machrihanish, hard against a beautiful sandy bay. Here, too, is all of the majesty of the West of Scotland (pastureland rising gently to hills and moor) and mysterious islands across a great rich, deep blue sea— Islay with its long fall down to the water and Jura, like some huge serpent arching towards the sky."
—Pat Ward-Thomas, *The Long Green Fairway* (1966)

It has been a little more than 30 years since my first visit to Scotland in June 1994. The sense of anticipation and excitement was tangible as I drove our rented Vauxhall Senator out of Glasgow Airport and onto the M8. My dad was fumbling with the Ordnance Survey map of Western Scotland while we searched for the Erskine Bridge over the Clyde—the route to Loch Lomond and ultimately Kintyre.

Miraculously, in the ancient age before we all carried supercomputers in our pockets, we found the Erskine off ramp and headed north to the A82. It was a relief to exit the hectic M8 and into somewhat calmer traffic. Before we knew it, we were out of the city and the stunning, mythical loch was on our right. It was a challenge to keep my eyes on the road with my father exclaiming, "Look at that!" every two minutes.

At Tarbet, we turned west on the A83. It was early afternoon when we reached Inverary. The scene is as vivid in my mind as if it happened yesterday. It was a clear day, not a cloud in the sky. We crossed over an ancient single lane arched bridge and saw the stark white Inverary Inn facing the shimmering blue water of Loch Fyne. A beautifully manicured community green sat between the hotel and the water.

"Let's stop here and get a drink," I said.

We found a shop and got coffee, then walked across the road and sat on a bench facing the loch and mountains beyond. The scene was like a James Guthrie painting come to life. I had no idea of the revelations that still awaited us down the road.

It was all south from here. First along the length of Loch Fyne, through Lochgilphead, Ardrishaig, Kennacraig, stopping in Tarbert for a late lunch. We were in Kintyre now. Just past the village of Clachan, which had a petrol station—rare for the day—we rounded a sharp curve and the world exploded. The entire horizon was taken over by the sparkling Atlantic Ocean. It was not blue; it was blindingly white—the small island of Gigha a greenish-black oasis.

The next several miles wound circuitously along the rocky coastline, interspersed with fields of sheep and massive black cows that were wedged between the road and the beach. Past Bellochantuy, the road turned suddenly inland towards Campbeltown—the original whisky capital of the world. Finally, a small sign on Main Street signaled the turnoff to Machrihanish on the B842. I don't know how my dad felt, but I almost felt dizzy at this point—almost to Machrihanish! The road passed relatively straight through lovely farmland for a few miles before a slight curve once again revealed the Atlantic. To our right, the brownish green linksland of *Machaire Shanish* tumbled down to the rocky beach.

We had not seen another car for several minutes. I stopped on the road to take in the incredible scene. There was a small, square, white hut on a rise in the distance, which I knew from my research was Ken Campbell's pro shop. It was located next to the mythical 1st tee, right above the beach. I will never forget the feeling of seeing a true Scottish links for the first time. I did not know it then, but the way I viewed golf would never be the same.

*To the Linksland*, Michael Bamberger's classic 1992 book, had inspired me to visit Machrihanish. The course was then largely unknown outside of Scotland. You could argue that it was not even known extensively *in* Scotland. This great, wild, natural links became my portal into the soul of Scottish golf. Almost as an afterthought, near the end of our visit, I was introduced to nearby Dunaverty Golf Club—a course that I had never heard of. The long afternoon I spent in Southend started me on a 30-year journey across the wondrous expanse of Scotland—in search of a game that was more about the people, the landscape, the culture, and the outrageously wild, outlandishly fun golf to be found in seemingly every corner of the country.

After we left Kintyre, we spent several days in St. Andrews, playing The Old Course and Carnoustie—a lifetime dream realized for my father. We made the trip up the coast to Cruden Bay, once again because of *To the Linksland*. After playing that mighty links all day, we drove back to St. Andrews that same night—earning an incredulous look from our bed and breakfast host.

One afternoon while strolling around St. Andrews, I walked into the old Quarto Bookshop. The distinctive, wonderful smell of old antiquarian books filled the air. Two hours passed in an instant. I found a copy of *Golf in My Gallowses* by Angus MacVicar, which I bought because it seemed to be about Dunaverty. I bought as many old golf books as I could reasonably hope to carry home.

On the counter, by an antique cash register, there were a few new books on display. One title, *Hell's Golfer* by Tom Morton, caught my eye. After a quick perusal, I decided I must have it. On the plane ride home to Alabama, Morton introduced me to the world of Carradale, Askernish, Isle of Harris and others—he had even visited Dunaverty in the book. I became obsessed with visiting places like this to search for what is authentic and elemental in this game—what is still unchanged after more than 250 years.

Over the course of 15 trips, I have played 108 golf courses in Scotland. I have been fortunate to stay for as long as three or four weeks on several of these visits—which has given me the time to explore places that are not easy to get to—like the otherworldly moonscape of the northwest Highlands or gloriously isolated islands in the Outer Hebrides. These 30 years of wandering my favorite country have convinced me that these 18 courses represent golf as it is meant to be played—as a birthright open to all, to meet good people, to walk in stunning natural landscapes, and to hit crazy, fun shots the way I did when I was 12 years old. They will allow you to recapture the joy you felt when you first fell in love with the game. These courses, for me, represent the living soul of golf.

This book was inspired by the 1951 classic *A Round of Golf Courses* by the English poet Patric Dickinson, a close friend of the great Bernard Darwin. Dickinson writes of his favorite 18 British courses with a style and elegance that sets the best golf writing apart from that of other sports. I aspire to honor that tradition. So now, let's go wandering.

The Ist. Tee, Corriecravie Golf Course

SANNOX GOLF COURSE, CORRIE
Copyright.
Cie, 20

# 1

## Aberfoyle

# Not All Who Wander Are Lost

> Come away, O human child!
>   To the waters and the wild
>   With a faery hand in hand,
>   For the world's more full of weeping
>     than you can understand.
>   —William Butler Yeats, "The Stolen Child" (1889)

In 1691 the minister of Aberfoyle, Robert Kirk, wrote a curious treatise called *The Secret Commonwealth of Elves, Fauns and Fairies*. The esoteric and remarkable work is a manifesto on the inhabitants of a magical fairy world, which Kirk—the seventh son of a seventh son—believed existed in an alternate realm of the Highlands. No copies of the original manuscript were known to be printed during the minister's lifetime. Less than a year after writing his seminal work, with his wife expecting a child, Reverend Robert Kirk passed away unexpectedly. It was finally published in 1815 at the request of legendary Scottish writer Sir Walter Scott.

It was one of Kirk's successors as Aberfoyle minister, Reverend Patrick Graham, who called his story to the attention of Sir

Walter. Graham believed that Kirk never actually died but was abducted by the faerie folk—for revealing their arcane ways and secrets to the human world. According to Graham's writings, Kirk suddenly appeared at the baptism of his youngest child and asked his brother-in-law to throw a silver dagger over his head to release him from fairyland. His request was refused, and he remained trapped forever in the world of the Fae. It is not known if there are golf courses in that magical realm.

The woodlands, lochs and glens of the Trossachs region, in which Aberfoyle lies, is a magical landscape lying to the east of mighty Ben Lomond. The world of this quintessentially Scottish golf course is a miniature version of the larger Trossachs landscape—Scots pines, larches, ancient oaks, old stone walls, heather, and gorse. Native plants explode in colors of purple, blue, red, yellow and endless shades of green. A three hour walk in this lovely, enthralling terrain with a few clubs and balls will help you understand why Reverend Robert Kirk was so desperate to return home. While I'm sure the land of faeries has its own occult wonders, they must pale in comparison to the natural beauty of Aberfoyle Golf Club.

On Boxing Day in 1890, a meeting was held at Aberfoyle Slate Companies, LTD for those interested in forming a golf club associated with a seven-hole course that had been laid out in the fields of a Mr. Gardner of Braeval, just outside of town. His Grace, the Duke of Montrose, was elected as the first club captain and the annual subscription was set at £10. In 1892, the club was extended to nine holes, and the membership grew to 42. Ladies were not charged to play the course. The club was first listed in the 1892 edition of *The Golfing Annual*:

> "The course, which consists of nine holes, with excellent hazards, is one mile from Aberfoyle railway station, and capital accommodation may be had at Bailie Nicol Jarvie Hotel, within three minutes' walk of the station. The view of the glens and lochs at the foot of Ben Lomond is very fine and is certainly an

What makes Scottish golf so matchless? Yes, there are the famous links situated on some of the rarest ground on earth. The high cathedrals of golf in Scotland—The Old Course, Prestwick, Dornoch, Muirfield, and Troon—are names known to anyone who has more than just a casual relationship with the game. For me, however, what sets Caledonian golf apart are the smaller, hidden courses—not on the way to anywhere—like Gairloch, Carradale, Leadhills, Whiting Bay and Aberfoyle. Places that take a special effort to reach. Places that reward that extra effort with golf in its purest and most unadulterated form.

The people of these proud, smaller clubs are a large part of their charm. As a visitor, especially a foreign one, you are likely to be treated like royalty. There is genuine concern from local members that you have fun and enjoy their course. This is not something that can be faked. It is sincere and real. It is the Scottish way. Aberfoyle is the perfect example of this ancient, and still extant, way.

The game is still played here for the same reason as it was on those original seven holes in 1890—to be around friendly people in a gloriously remote natural setting, walking and playing on a quirky, joy-inducing layout. Many times, this remoteness, while

wonderful, is a handicap. Aberfoyle is clearly not on the way to anywhere the ordinary golfing visitor chooses to travel. Only an hour's drive north of Glasgow Airport, it feels like another world altogether. Time is so precious on a golf trip in Scotland. It takes a commitment to get to Aberfoyle.

On my first visit to Aberfoyle in August 2023, I drove straight to the course after 24 hours of travel—dodging international cyclists competing in the Road World Championship the entire way—to meet current club captain and treasurer William Paterson for a game. Paterson, a Glaswegian through and through, loves everything about the course. He was a longtime member before joining a club closer to his home, only to return several years ago to Aberfoyle.

"I think it's brilliant. It can be infuriating, and relentless at punishing slightly off shots, but no two holes are the same. If you look at the scorecard, you may think it's all going to be the same, as there are a lot of 300-375 yard par-four holes. How can this be a challenge? However, once you play the course you soon realize that the 3rd is nothing like the 7th and the 7th is nothing like the 15th. As someone who isn't a big hitter, it gives you a chance to put a good score together. The slopes give you difficult stances, and the small greens are difficult to hit or to chip on should you miss them. Add to all that the glorious setting and it just makes it somewhere to love. Shouldn't that be the way—a course that everyone can play and enjoy regardless of handicap, but one that is equally a challenge to all? I'd like to think we are the epitome of the local Scottish course," says Paterson.

The lovely, well-kept, clubhouse was currently not offering any catering—a symptom of the existential challenges that clubs like Aberfoyle face. "We've had a number of caterers try, but we don't have enough traffic from golfers just now," my new friend said as he handed me a bag full of Scottish delicacies—an Orange Fanta, a cheese and onion sandwich, salt and vinegar crisps, and Tunnock's tea cakes. He was worried, correctly, that I would not have had time for lunch in the mad rush from the airport. William's thoughtfulness immediately put me back in a Scottish frame of mind. Having visited the country for most of my adult life, I can confidently say that Scots are the best people on earth.

My wife and I were meant to stay in Oban for the night, with a late dinner reservation at the highly rated EE-USK. After we played the brilliant par-three 10th—an intricate, perfect jewel of a hole—my adrenaline started to wear off, and my legs began to fail. Thinking of the drive still ahead of us, I regretfully begged off the rest of our game. The course had immediately struck me as delightful—with a blind approach shot to a superb punch bowl green at the 1st. The 4th through the 10th were one delightfully quirky hole after another. I vowed to come back on my next trip and play the entire 18-hole layout.

After our 10-hole game, William and I drove into town to meet our wives. His wife had generously offered to take mine into Aberfoyle for tea while we played golf. In the car park, he insisted that we take The Duke's Pass—one of the most scenic drives in the country—to get from Aberfoyle over towards Callander and then on to Oban. Built in 1885 as an estate road by the Duke of Montrose, it was later improved to serve Victorian tourists who came to the area after Sir Walter Scott's epic poem about Loch Katrine, "The Lady of the Lake," was published. After a few minutes on the impossibly winding mountain road, I noticed a car behind us. William and his wife had followed us out of town for a few miles—in the opposite direction of their home in Glasgow—just to make sure we were on the right path.

Though not all that far from the urban center of Glasgow, Aberfoyle feels as if it's a million miles away, both in distance and time. Most of the holes on the front nine are from the original 1890 layout in a farmer's grazing land. There is a feeling that you are playing the game as it would have been played by the Duke of Montrose in the first monthly medal. The location is both a blessing and a curse. Paterson is characteristically direct in assessing the challenges facing the club:

> "We clearly need more members—there are currently around 135 adult members. The town and the local area aren't populated enough, so we need to attract members who are willing to travel. When we had a membership of over 500, we had lots of members travelling from lots of different areas—up from Glasgow or across from Stirling and Dunblane. The price of fuel, the dwindling membership, and the lack of catering/bar make it difficult for us. We also need an increase in visitors' numbers and income. At £40 for a day ticket, I think we are very good value. How do we get people to come to our course? I think it's a travesty that the course is so under-utilized. The Trossachs is a popular tourist area—but mainly for walkers and hikers, due to the incredible scenery. We get the occasional casual tourist golfer, but it's not an area known for golf tourism. It's difficult to attract golfers to come here when there are so many alternatives in Scotland."

In July 2024, I returned to Aberfoyle with my son Jake. Near the end of a two-week trip around Scotland, we drove down from Aberdeen on a lovely Friday evening. We were met by Paterson and club secretary Bob Carmichael, who were waiting at a picnic table in front of the clubhouse. William had booked us for the evening at the Black Bull Pub in the nearby village of Gartmore. It was decided we would play the front nine before dinner and then come back in the morning for the back nine. It was a good plan.

Once again, the blind punchbowl 1st green made me smile. Jake was immediately taken with Aberfoyle. "This place is great, Dad," he said as we waited for a moment on the sheltered 2nd tee. As they had the year before, Holes 4 through 10 struck me as an ideal example of inland Scottish golf. Jake was incredulous at the mostly deserted golf course:

"Can you imagine a place like this in Alabama on a nice Friday afternoon? There would be 200 people playing."

A few holes deserve special mention. The 4th, called Alma, is a 256-yard, wildly uphill, par four that will find a place in my next ranking of the Top 100 holes in Scotland. The tiny, bizarre, brilliant green, is benched into the side of the hill overlooking the dramatic countryside. From the fairway below, it looks impossible to hit. Most golfers lay back from the tee and take their chances with a wedge. As if by magic, my 80-yard approach hit the steep backstop and rolled to a foot from the hole. I think William's excitement was greater than mine.

"That's a wonderful birdie, Jim! It must be one of the best of your trip," exclaimed our host.

"Well, there isn't too much competition in that category, if I'm being honest," I replied.

The peak of Ben Lomond looms powerfully in the distance on the wonderful 5th and 6th, both testing par-three holes. Benches are thoughtfully placed at each tee, encouraging golfers to spare a moment for the stunning scenery. Fairy Knowe, the 305-yard 7th, is another standout. It is a 90-degree dogleg left that requires a precise mid-iron layup to set up an approach that is the pure nectar of Scottish golf. As you stand in this fairway, surrounded by all the vibrant colors of nature, it would not be much of a shock to see one of the denizens of the enchanted fairy world make an appearance.

Our thoughts began to turn to a pint of Tennent's at the Black Bull as we walked off the 9th. The 10th at Aberfoyle, however, is one of the great short holes in Scotland. William wisely suggested that we play it before stopping for the night. "This way you can play it again in the morning," he said. It was good advice. This is one of those idyllic short par threes that exist throughout the country—like the 4th at Dunaverty, the 2nd at Corrie, the 12th at Hopeman, the 7th at Gairloch, or the 9th at Durness. A book could be written about these holes alone.

Roderick, as the hole is called, is only 123-yards. Everything about it seems to be taken from an 1890s watercolor by the Glasgow Boys. There is a winding, musical burn bordered by colorful native plants. There is an old stone wall in play, right next to the green. Late in the evening, the larch-covered hillside beyond looks like the Old Forest from Tolkien's Shire. Whenever I start to tell someone about Aberfoyle, the first photo I show them is of this hole.

We went to our room at the nearby Rob Roy Hotel to clean up for dinner. William was waiting with a pint for each of us in the hotel bar. As golfers have done for centuries, we recounted the highlights of the day, both good and bad. He kindly offered to drive us to the Black Bull Pub, where we spent one of the most wonderful nights of our entire trip. The evening had cooled drastically. The warm, bright interior of the old building, which dates to the 17th century, could not have been more welcoming. Over a long, excellent meal, we discussed Scottish bands of the 80s and 90s—The Blue Nile, The Cocteau Twins, Teenage Fanclub. Jake and William had just met a few hours earlier, but they debated the relative merits of these seminal groups like two old music professors. It was one of those evenings that nobody wanted to end. Golf is the greatest game because of the people I've met.

Bob Carmichael dutifully met us at the club early the next morning. He had come out on a Saturday to walk the course with another member, Brian Maitland, to fill divots. We played the 10th again, now in the early morning mist. Not much was said as we all hit our shots. I hung back for a moment on the tee and watched Jake walk towards the green, carrying his bag. I suddenly felt so happy that he had been able to come over to Scotland again with me.

The back nine at Aberfoyle is also a joy, though it is a bit more difficult to walk. The 15th and 17th, shortish par fours, are the two standouts for me. They are wonderful, inherently Scottish, affairs with blind shots and bells. What more do you need?

The original 9th hole from 1890 is now the 18th. It is a beautiful downhill par four and a fitting climax to this delightful course. The original wee clubhouse still stands, precariously, right beside the green. Unfortunately, this perfectly scaled Victorian structure is slowly falling into ruin. It could perhaps still be saved, but it is near the point of no return. The club is just trying to survive, so I do not fault them for this. Still, I can't help but imagine this lovely little building restored to its former glory. I know an architect that would work on it for free.

We said our goodbyes at the picnic table. Bob and Brian were taking a break from the Saturday morning divot maintenance. Jake and William promised to continue their wide-ranging musical discussion by e-mail. I looked out over the A81 to the mountains beyond, near Callander. Cows and sheep stood frozen in the quiet glen, all facing the same direction—as if expecting a message from the mythical world of fairies. Comrie and St Fillans, I thought, lie on the other side of those hills. We are lucky that there are still such places in the world. The world needs places like Aberfoyle.

The "freedom to roam" the countryside is a birthright here. Golf is part of that heritage. Wander off the beaten path and spend £40 on a day ticket. Yes, time is precious—but you will not regret it. Not all who wander are lost.

Shiskine Golf Course and Drumadoon Point

# 2

## Anstruther

# To Our Glorious Dead

"Hear my soul speak. The very instant that I saw
you, did my heart fly at your service."
—William Shakespeare, *Coriolanus*

A couple of days before embarking on a dream golf trip to Scotland with my son Jake in 2019, I had set a 4 a.m. calendar alert to enter the online ballot for a tee time at the Old Course. I soon found out the course was closed for visitor play for the entire duration of our visit to Fife. I was worried that my poor planning would ruin the trip for my son. As it turned out, it was a blessing in disguise. On the day we had planned on trying to play the most famous course in golf, we instead drove a short distance south of St Andrews to Anstruther Golf Club. We put our green fee in an honesty box and proceeded to play all day on a wild Old Tom Morris nine-hole layout by the ocean.

The town of Anstruther, about 20 minutes southeast of St Andrews, has everything you could wish for on a Scottish holiday. It's a beautiful seaside village with pubs, shops, restaurants—all easily walkable—and with the first tee of a brilliant golf course right in the middle of it all. Golf has been played on the links at Anstruther Golf Club, originally known as Billowness, since 1890.

We showed up at Anstruther Golf Club around 8:30 a.m. to find the clubhouse was locked, except for one door leading into a small vestibule outside of the locker rooms. Nobody was around, except for one local member about to go out alone. Perhaps sensing my confusion, he said, "Normally you pay in the bar, but they don't get here until 10. Just put your money in the wee honesty box and go play."

We had no idea what to expect, but almost every hole was memorable and fun. How often can you recall every hole in detail after only playing a course once? Anstruther is that kind of place. We played all day. When we came in for lunch after our first 27 holes, I asked the helpful bar manager if I should give her any more money to play all day. She looked a bit confused.

"All day? Oh, I don't know, just give me 10 more pounds to cover the both of you."

When I told her how much we loved the golf course, she immediately handed each of us an Anstruther ball marker.

In recent years there has been a growing acceptance of golf courses that do not conform to the standard norms of modern design. The idea that a course must have a certain mixture of long and short holes to be a real test of golf has come under welcome scrutiny. In Tom Doak's seminal golf architecture book *The Confidential Guide to Golf Courses*, courses around the world are rated on a scale of 1-10. Throughout the book, nine-hole courses like Anstruther, or even a beloved 12-hole course like Shiskine, are often dismissed out of hand with ratings as low as 2. On the Doak Scale, a rating of 2 is described as "A mediocre golf course with little or no architectural interest, but nothing really horrible. Play it in a scramble and drink a lot of beer." For reference, he also rates the great Dunaverty Golf Club as a 2. Anstruther Golf Club would be a 10 on the Hartsell Scale. It's telling that *The Confidential Guide to Golf Courses* does not include Anstruther Golf Club. This is perhaps for the best. There are enough courses rated a "2" in it already.

Par is largely irrelevant in Scotland. Golf is entirely dependent on the conditions of the day. It may take two good shots to reach a par three or one good shot to reach a par four. This is especially true on a totally exposed headland course like Anstruther. The main objective in golf is to get the ball in the hole in fewer strokes than your opponent. Given this fact, does it really matter if a course is a par 31, 66, or 72? Any golfer would be pleased to go around Anstruther in level fours. It has a quirky mix of golf holes—with four par fours and five par threes for a total par of 31.

As we stood on the 1st tee, it was easy to see that a special day is imminent. It is a scene that is unique in the world of golf. The green sits on a plateau about 40 feet above the tee level next to an imposing granite monument, with a plaque that reads "To Our Glorious Dead". It was originally dedicated to the local heroes of World War I. The gray cenotaph has silently watched over the links since 1920. Leave it to the Scots to place an important monument on a golf course, where it is sure to be seen and remembered.

Play at Anstruther is dictated by the wind. On the day of our visit, it was steady at 15-20 mph, which I imagine is probably the standard velocity. This gentle breeze completely changed direction between our morning 27 and afternoon 18, resulting in a very different golf course in the evening. Before lunch, the first hole played downwind. The steep plateau could be reached with a well struck driver, leaving a traditional Scottish run-up shot to the green as the correct play. After lunch, the wind changed direction and the hill could not be carried, rendering the 2nd shot blind and vastly more difficult. Playing downwind, this 270-yard par four is an opportunity for a birdie. It is one of the few relatively easy chances on the course.

Once the summit of the 1st is reached, the joys of the Old Tom Morris designed headland links are fully revealed. The golfer can be forgiven for pausing a moment to take it all in—the town of Anstruther sweeping away below, the monument and the rocky shores of the Atlantic. The 2nd—a 160-yarder aptly named Monument—plays straight out to the ocean in a strong crosswind.

The green is sited on the edge of the cliff with the expanse of the sea as a backdrop; a memorable and testing par three. Headland golf in Scotland is a special pleasure.

The 3rd and 4th, both par fours, play on top of the plateau. The 3rd is a longish hole at 402 yards, has fairway bunkers to be avoided, but with the helping wind plays much shorter than its longer successor. The 4th hole, Magazine, is an excellent par four. It plays along the clifftop, with the ocean on the right, usually straight into the prevailing wind. There is safety to the left. However, in taking the cautious route off the tee, the approach must be played over an old stone wall and remnants of a World War I arsenal building used for the storage of ammunition. The correct angle is down the right side of the fairway, but this brings the cliff into the equation. Whether you are bold or hesitant off the tee, the green seems to float above the ocean below. This is the Scottish golf of our dreams. Jake was hooked immediately, almost running between shots like a 5-year-old kid does.

Rockies, the 5th hole, is a one-off in the world of golf. A blind dogleg 247-yard par three played from a clifftop to the clouds. A plaque by the tee proudly notes that it was once voted the toughest par three in the U.K. by *Golf Monthly*. I later asked an old member in the bar if he thought it really is the toughest par three in the country, "Oh aye," he replied, "because it's a par four."

Most members do treat the hole as a par four. Many of the older men, and a lot of the ladies, play back down the 4th fairway to pitch straight down onto the green from the upper level. We played the hole five times, and I still do not know how the green could be hit in regulation. There is a smallish strip of fairway on the beach level, where the green sits. A potential lay-up shot could be played there. A bogey on this hole feels like a very good score. It is a beautiful, bizarre, and preposterously fun golf hole.

The 6th hole is another wonderful par three with the green sited on the lower level at the base of the cliffside. It plays 128 yards from both the lower Members tee, as well as from the much more dramatic Medal tee on top of the hill. In our ignorance, we had started our first nine of the day playing from the Medal tees.

Climbing back down from this extraordinary tee, we were caught red-handed by the greenskeeper, who had shown up to work on the 5th green.

"You shouldn't be playing the Medal tees," he said sternly.

"I'm sorry, it's our first visit here and there was nobody in the clubhouse when we started," I said embarrassingly.

He smiled and said, "Aye. In that case, I'm glad you got to see the view from up there but keep to the yellow tees for the rest of the day."

The tee shot to the 171-yard, par-three 7th hole plays back over the 6th fairway to a green located back on the upper headland. I hit a full driver on this hole in three of our five rounds. Par must be a winner in virtually every match. The 8th is the only pedestrian hole on the course, basically serving to get us from the 7th green to the 9th tee. The closing hole is a 230-yard par three, playing back into town from the previously scaled heights of the 1st green. It is a unique and dramatic finishing hole, great for match play. Like the 5th, it plays more like a par four, reinforcing one final time that par is but a theoretical construct in Scotland.

Matt Maclachlan, then the Clubhouse Manager for over 10 years at Anstruther, came to our table to visit as we perused the bar menu. He was genuinely interested in our feelings about the course and introduced us to a few of the members who were in for an afternoon pint. A grand Scottish tradition, and one that applies at almost every one of the 18 courses in this book, is that people are genuinely interested in your thoughts about their course. We had a lively discussion about how to play the 5th and where to get the best fish and chips in Anstruther. Matt told us what makes Anstruther so special to him:

> "Everyone that walks through the door here gets afforded the same welcome, as if we've known you all our life. Whether it's a member, visitor or just someone visiting the restaurant, our aim is to have people say to themselves as they leave, 'well we will definitely be coming back here' and 99 percent of the time it works."

A more welcoming golf club cannot be found.

We only visited Anstruther by chance that day, because we missed out on playing The Old Course. This might seem an impossible blow to overcome at the beginning of a Scottish golf trip. Instead, Anstruther Golf Club became a highlight of my son's first trip to Scotland.

After playing all morning and into the afternoon, Jake asked me to cancel our 2:30 pm round at Lundin Links. He did not want to leave Anstruther. We went back out for 18 more holes after lunch. Walking off the 9th green, after our 45th hole of the day, I could tell my son wanted to keep playing. There was still enough daylight left for nine more holes, but my old legs were gone. As I shook his hand in the lingering Scottish twilight, he said, "This is the most fun I've ever had playing golf."

# 3

# Askernish

## Aisgernis, mo chride

On—and at nightfall at last
Come to the end of our way,
To the lonely inn 'mid the rocks;
Where the gaunt and taciturn host
Stands on the threshold
    —Matthew Arnold, "Rugby Chapel" (1857)

Quests often end in disappointment. Things that are built up in our mind, over time, rarely live up to expectations. We spend years searching in vain for that elusive treasure, only to come up disappointed. And yet, if you're lucky, maybe a few times in your life, you can find a place that surpasses even your highest hopes.

The small, tidy clubhouse at Askernish Golf Club consists of two large rooms. Four sets of ancient-looking hickory golf clubs stood neatly in the corner of the well-stocked shop. The warm interior offered a momentary respite from the ravages of the cold Atlantic wind. My three previous attempts to reach the near-mythical course on the Isle of South Uist had failed, due to the vagaries of travel logistics. Over the years, getting to this place had become something of a personal quest. My friend Robbie Wilson and I had our travel challenges on the way, but we had made it. A friendly man called Aeneas Bremner took our green fees, along with payment for a generous amount of club merchandise. With our golf transactions complete, I asked Aeneas for dinner recommendations. His response was wonderfully direct:

"You'll be going to the Politician on Eriskay tonight. That's all there is to it. What time would you like a table?

I looked at my traveling companion for an answer. "6 p.m. would be great," he said.

"Perfect. I'll book it for you now. Enjoy your round."

This type of reception is common throughout the Outer Hebrides. People on this chain of small islands display warmth and openness that belies their almost complete isolation from the often frantic, chaotic world of the mainland.

The island of South Uist possesses a stark, gaunt, natural beauty. It is connected to the smaller islands of Benbecula and Eriskay by a series of rocky causeways. Prior to the construction of the causeways, the only access between the string of islands was by ferry. Askernish, on the southern tip of the island, is exposed to the full fury of the Atlantic Ocean. The next land is 2,000 miles to the west, in North America. It's a place where you feel gloriously secluded from the rest of the planet. We heard the ancient language of Gaelic being spoken in the local Co-Op when we stopped to buy a Lucozade.

The saga of the rediscovery of the lost links of Askernish has been well documented. Seminal stories by John Garrity ("A Journey to the Western Isles," in *Sports Illustrated*, 1991) and David Owen ("The Ghost Course," in *The New Yorker*, 2009) are essential reading. The original course was laid out in 1891 by Old Tom Morris, at the request of wealthy landowner Lady Emily Cathcart, for the use of her guests. At the time, her family owned the islands of South Uist, Benbecula, and Barra. They were called Lairds.

It's believed that the original Old Tom course was abandoned in the 1920s. Regardless of the exact date, it was quickly reclaimed by nature. For many years, the land was used solely for crofting. In the 1970s, a nine-hole course was laid out on the adjacent *machair*—a fecund, sandy grassland that exists only on the west coast of Scotland and a few places in Ireland. The turf of the machair is springy and resilient: a rare landscape that is ideal for golf. The only remnant of that nine-hole course is the current 18th green. Today, Holes 1 through 5, and the 18th, are located on the machair and share it with grazing cattle. They are very good holes, but the natural majesty of Askernish is to be found in the heaving and mighty dunes of Holes 6 through 17. This run of holes recalls the front nine at Cruden Bay or Machrihanish—or parts of Royal Portrush—but with a much longer stretch of holes in the natural dune land. It is wild, natural golf.

While on a tour of the western islands and Outer Hebrides with Robbie, who lives in Lochgilphead, we first visited the holy Island of Iona. The golf course there is itself a natural wonder. Iona Abbey is also a special place, a mecca for many people. But it's not easy to get from Iona to Askernish. The journey was a logistical puzzle, involving at least three ferries. Our 11 a.m. Uig to Lochboisdale sailing was canceled at 5 p.m. the night before. My third attempt to reach this mythical links was suddenly in serious jeopardy.

Fortunately, Robbie is a canny and determined Scot. He presented our case to a sympathetic and helpful Caledonian Macbrayne operator. She was able to reschedule us on the 4 p.m. boat from Uig to Lochmaddy on North Uist. This would necessitate a relatively long, late-night drive, but we would be able to reach our destination. In the dim gray twilight, we drove down the A865 from Lochmaddy to Lochboisdale. On the Isle of Benbecula, a herd of massive red deer slowly crossed the single carriageway, no more than 50 yards in front of us. It was a surreal and beautiful vision, like an ethereal landscape scene from *A Thin Red Line.*

We were scheduled to play Askernish at 9 a.m. the next day with Colin Russell, then the club captain. It was a dark and foreboding Sunday morning when we arrived at the tidy, locked clubhouse. Nobody was about. We huddled on the front porch to escape the brutal western wind. The greenskeeper arrived soon after us. He rode his mower through the gate out onto the machair. His dog was leading the way, sprinting with the enthusiasm of an excited child.

Colin arrived dutifully at 8:40, driving down from his home in the village of Balranald on North Uist. After our initial introductions, I said, "Please do not feel obligated to go out in this weather with us. You do not have to suffer through this." The rain was blowing sideways.

"Don't be daft, Jim. You are here and we are playing. If I only played golf in perfect weather, I wouldn't play very much at all," said the friendly club captain.

This kind gesture enhanced our round exponentially. Colin was an ideal host, giving us the history of the holes and pointing out the correct lines on every shot. He played golf cross-handed, quite efficiently, which I found to be amazing. When I mentioned this to Robbie, he was not surprised in the least, attributing it to the influence of Shinty in western Scotland.

The rain and wind momentarily subsided for the first five holes, which are sited on the smooth, ancient machair. Askernish lulls you into a false sense of security. These pleasant, gently rolling holes are a perfect—and somewhat misleading—introduction for what is to come. The lovely turf was dotted with small daisies. Cattle grazed by the greens, unconcerned at our presence. It was all lovely and fun, but far from awe inspiring.

This changed abruptly when we reached the 7th tee. Here, the course enters the realm of the fantastic. A 438-yard par four called Cabinet Minister, it is routed in a narrow valley through massive dunes. We can only speculate on the distant past, but it's easy to imagine Old Tom Morris standing on this tee and seeing a great hole in front of him. As you walk through the valley, there is an even greater sense of isolation from the larger world.

Adam Lawrence, the editor of *Golf Course Architecture* magazine, was a part of the now famous initial visit to South Uist in March 2006 with architect Martin Ebert, Gordon Irvine, Chris Haspell, and club chairman Ralph Thompson. He eloquently recalls that first, thrilling trip to Askernish:

> "As we flew northwest, the weather started to break.
> I remember getting a really good view of Skye, a place
> I love. By the time we landed in Benbecula, it was to-
> tally clear, albeit very cold—pretty much the Platonic
> form of a Scottish late winter or early spring day. A
> friendly, burly man, called Ralph Thompson, then the
> club chairman, met us at the airport and drove us to
> the golf course. There was nothing there, once you
> passed Askernish House, the old laird's house. There
> was a gate that led onto the machair. Ralph drove us
> out onto the grass and stopped at the foot of what
> we later learned was the seawall dune. The land was
> open, obviously a links, but rather flat and frankly
> nothing very special. He then walked us fifteen or
> twenty yards south, and the world changed. We were
> standing on what is now the 7th tee, with the huge
> dune valley in front of us, and nothing but other
> enormous dunes as far as the eye could see. Martin
> said to me quietly, "Well this has suddenly become the
> most interesting project on the books." Very little else
> was said, we were too awed."

This sense of awe only intensifies as you play the 8th, 9th, and 10th, a triumvirate of natural links par fours that sit perfectly in the native landscape. The penalty for missing a fairway or green is steep, but every shot is thrilling and fun. The steep climb from the 10th green to the 11th tee brings us to the most memorable hole at Askernish: Barra Sight.

This 193-yard par three plays uphill, across a deep chasm, to a completely hidden green. There appears to be no safe direction to hit the ball. All that is visible is the wild and churning Atlantic. Stephen Proctor, author of the remarkable trilogy of golf history—*Monarch of the Green*, *The Long Golden Afternoon*, and *Matchless*—has made the sacred pilgrimage to South Uist. He visited in 2021 to help promote the creation of the Old Tom Morris Trail, a grouping of Scottish golf courses with a design connection to the great man of Scottish golf. The club named him as an Honorary Life Member during his visit, an honor he considers one of the greatest of his life. The 11th hole left a lasting impression on the American writer:

> "I thought the 11th was the single most dramatic hole at Askernish. The tee is on this massive dune and you can't see the green at all. You just guess it's somewhere out in front of you. The wind is just howling from the ocean—straight across. To the left of the green, everywhere, behind the green, off to the left, literally to the right—everything is perdition, just absolute disaster. Except for a small strip of land out in front of the green that you don't even know is there. You just hope and pray that when the wind carries your ball back, as inevitably it must. You hope it will land in some place where you have another shot."

As we stood on the 11th tee, the howling wind, coming straight off the ocean at 35 mph, threatened to blow us over. The sideways rain was like a swarm of angry bees. I cannot imagine the hole ever playing as anything less than a full driver for the average golfer. Our host told us about the hidden strip of fairway, but that was not very reassuring. My tee shot flew onto the beach, and I climbed down to play it, with Colin eyeing me skeptically. Barra Sight is high in my pantheon of heroic and dramatic golf holes.

The spiritual heart of Askernish is the dune ridge, high above the beach, between the 11th green and 12th tee. We stood there in silence for a few moments in the raging wind and took in the entire scene. A pair of lovely memorial benches are placed in this perfect spot. The entire links was shrouded in a heavy, gray mist.

We were so wet that any further protection from the elements was pointless. Despite these conditions, or maybe in some way because of them, it was a vista unlike anything I have seen.

The 12th hole is a serious challenge. It's 582 yards long and plays away from the ocean. By some form of eldritch magic only found in the Outer Hebrides, the wind had completely changed direction and was now straight into us. From the elevated tee I hit a good drive, followed by a three-wood, another three-wood, and then a full five iron, before holing out a 40-yard running pitch for a par. It has to rank with the greatest scores I have ever made on a single hole. It is impossible to describe how tough this hole is.

The greens at Askernish are natural and wildly undulating wonders. Hole after hole, Robbie would inevitably say, "Look at that, Jim" or just simply, "wow." The 15th green stands out for me. It's a naturally sited, submerged punchbowl, and the approach is largely blind. The weather was relenting a bit, so I took the opportunity to hit a few chip shots onto the various slopes of the green. I could have spent an hour playing shots into this lovely work of art.

A note about the constant rain we faced—the turf at Askernish played firm and fast despite it. The machair drains unlike any other natural landform—water just runs right through it.

Of the remaining holes, the 359-yard 16th, called Old Tom's Pulpit, is foremost in my memory. The wonderfully framed tee shot is played down into a narrow valley. A blind approach is uphill and over a dune, to a wildly sloping green that rivals—or even surpasses—the unique 15th green. It's the essence of a natural golf hole. You crest the dune on the 16th with a sense of excitement and anticipation. "I think Old Tom expected golf to be a giant drama," says Stephen Proctor.

Back in the shelter of the clubhouse, our faithful caretaker Aeneas offered us a much-needed warm drink. "You're all sorted for The Politician tonight," he said, handing me a coffee. We sat with Colin Russell and a few other members. They were genuinely interested in our thoughts on their golf course. I did not want to leave.

Later that evening, Robbie and I made the 15-minute drive over the causeway to Eriskay and The Politician. The hilarious 1949 movie *Whisky Galore* is loosely based on a novel by Compton MacKenzie about the 1941 wreck of the cargo ship the SS Politician, off the coast of Eriskay. The ship was carrying a cargo of bootleg whisky bound for the United States. Enterprising islanders took it upon themselves to salvage as much of the cargo as they could carry. They hid it from the authorities, all over the island, in caves and in crofts. There are several unopened bottles from the shipwreck on the backbar at The Politician.

An older gentleman was seated by himself at the corner stool in the bar. He immediately introduced himself as Paddy Forbes. We took a seat next to him and ordered a pint. Golfers seem to have a sixth sense about other golfers.

"Have you been playing at Askernish today?" asked our new friend. "I was club captain there. I still play as much as I can. What did you think of our wee course?"

We had some time before our table was ready. A wonderful meal awaited us; among the best I've ever had in Scotland. For the next hour, Paddy regaled us with tales of his beloved golf course and the true story of *Whisky Galore*. We told him how much we loved Askernish. I felt like I had discovered a treasure. It was the night of a lifetime.

A few weeks after our visit, Robbie messaged me that he had heard that Paddy passed away. *Bha deagh bheatha aige.*

## The Wee Clubhouses of Scotland

"Must not beauty, then, it will be asked, be sought for in the forms which we associate with our every-day life?"
—John Ruskin, *The Seven Lamps of Architecture* (1849)

In 1849, the English art theorist John Ruskin published a lengthy essay called *The Seven Lamps of Architecture.* This seminal work was the foundation of establishing "Victorian Gothic" as the prevalent architectural style in Britain for the next 70 years. Ruskin believed there were seven guiding principles of architecture: Sacrifice, Truth, Power, Beauty, Life, Memory, and Obedience. Looking back on these concepts through the lens of history, some of them are more relevant than others. Still pertinent today is the tenet of memory, which suggests that buildings should reflect the history and traditions of the local culture where they are created. Ruskin believed the average person has an inherent instinct for beauty. This is reflected in the simple, unassuming charm of the clubhouses at Corrie, Bute, Isle of Seil, and Traigh.

There are many iconic clubhouse buildings in golf—the Royal and Ancient, Shinnecock, Panmure, and Prestwick come quickly to mind. However, each of these are the work of well-known architects of the day. The wee clubhouses of Scotland reveal the *genius loci*—the spirit of the place. They were often the work of local craftsmen and created by people who worked in the local design vernacular. They reflect the joy, through unique simplicity, to be found in playing these remote nine-hole courses; places where the game remains as it was played in Scotland over 125 years ago. They reflect the smaller scale of the golfing experience—an honesty box, a brisk walk by the sea, enjoying a cup of tea or a tin of Tennent's amongst ancient mahogany millwork. They are a place to sit with a few friends, both old and new, recounting the best shots of the match. In these tiny chapels of golf, the troubles of the outside world can be nonexistent for a few precious moments.

Golf clubs are often the center of social activity in the small communities of Scotland. These humble structures offer only basic amenities: shelter from the elements, a place to rest, a physical location for essential club business. However, their elegant, honest unsophistication exemplifies something much larger than

these fundamental uses. Golf, at its heart, is about spending quality time with other people. Even the humblest sheds can enhance the joy of human interaction.

## — — — CORRIE — — —

Glen Sannox is a world unto itself. Located on Arran, an island that rises dramatically out of the Firth of Clyde between the Ayrshire coast and the Kintyre peninsula, it is framed by the imposing peaks of Cir Mhor and Goatfell. The Sannox Burn flows down from the mountains, through the glen, and out to the sea, providing a natural melodic soundtrack for the lush green valley. Golf was introduced to this secluded world in 1892. It was a time of massive growth in the game throughout Great Britain.

The nine holes of Corrie Golf Club were laid out by locals on the land of a Sannox farmer. The amateur golf course architects took full advantage of the dramatic ground to the east of the winding burn.

The course was first listed in Volume 5 of *The Golfing Annual* in 1892:

> "The course, of nine holes, is situated at the entrance
> of Glen Sannox, on the north side of the Sannox
> Burn. It is of a sporting nature, bunkers and hazards
> abounding, while the greens are fairly good, and, with
> the attention they are now getting, should soon be
> first rate."

A vibrant membership soon developed. In 1897, a local joiner was commissioned to construct a clubhouse near the 1st tee. Less than 60 miles away, the great Scottish architect Charles Rennie MacKintosh was working on the design of his masterpiece, The Glasgow School of Art building. No famous designer was needed at Corrie. It is easy to see the care that was taken to make this tiny building so special. The elegant lines of the small jewel box-like structure prove Ruskin's theory; that average working people have an inherent understanding of beauty.

The entrance into the Corrie car park from the narrow A841 is a testing one, even by Scottish standards. A mirror mounted on a tree near the sharp turn helps indicate oncoming traffic. Most of the vehicles are there for afternoon tea at Fran's Tea Room, where green fees can be paid and "burn balls" can be purchased for a mere 50p each, three for £1. The apple crumble with Arran ice cream is a tempting pre-round snack.

A small hunter-green colored structure, with a bright magenta corrugated metal roof and trim, sits next to the tearoom. It is no more than 1,000 square feet, adorned with simple Victorian style brackets and roof finials. An honesty box, for use when Fran's is closed, is mounted on the wall of a narrow porch with two built-in benches. A sign indicates the current green fees—£15 for nine holes, £25 for a day ticket. In the 1970s, two small lean-to additions were made to the original structure—a visitor's changing room and storage area.

There was a movement in the late 19th century to give the working class of Britain a more affordable chance to play the game. Many of the original Corrie members were workers from a nearby barytes mine. It is easy to imagine their pride when the

new clubhouse opened. Inside the burnished wood paneled locker room, time stands still. If you ignore the few implements of modern life, it could easily be 1897.

An old photograph recently found by the club shows the 1906 medal winner Alex Kerr standing proudly in front of the clubhouse with his bag of hickory clubs. The building in that grainy black and white photo is identical to the one that sits in Glen Sannox today. Thankfully, things change slowly, if ever, in the remote parts of Scotland. This elegant, unassuming structure will immediately bring a smile to a visitor's face. It sets the tone perfectly for the fun to come. All are welcome at Corrie.

## — — — BUTE — — —

The royal burgh of Rothesay on the Isle of Bute was a popular Victorian era tourist destination. Glasgow holiday goers flocked to the picturesque town on large paddle steamers. Golf came to the island in the late 1800s as part of the array of holiday activities. Rothesay Golf Club, a lost James Braid design, was constructed in the middle of town, along with a large community putting green that still sits next to the ferry terminal on Rothesay Bay. With the influx of visitors, local golfers decided that the island needed a proper seaside course. In 1888 the nine hole Bute Golf Club was laid out six miles south of Rothesay, in Kingarth, on rolling, sandy grazing land next to the Firth of Clyde.

As play at the club increased, a clubhouse was needed at the remote links. In 1911 the members celebrated the grand opening of a new "golf pavilion." A local Member of Parliament, Mr. Harry Hope, spoke at the gathering. According to the April 11th edition of *The Scotsman*, the MP gave a short speech referring to "the natural beauties of the course of the premier club in Bute" and that the site was "the ideal golf course." Afterwards, the ladies of the club "entertained the members and their guests to tea." It is not hard to picture them today, as the small, elegant Victorian pavilion has remained unchanged since that day.

The drive from Rothesay to Bute Golf Club winds along lovely cascading farmland or through the towering Scotch pines of the coastal road, depending on your choice of route. Of the two options, one is more likely to have sheep in the carriageway than oncoming cars. It is just as well. This is not a drive to be rushed. Along the seaside path, the Victorian Gothic architectural masterpiece, Mount Stuart, sits on 3,000 acres on the Firth of Clyde. It is worth a break from golf to spend an afternoon walking the grounds of this remarkable estate, now operated by the Historic Trust of Scotland. It is the ancestral home of the descendants of King Robert II of Scotland.

Just before reaching the small village of Kingarth, a sign for Bute Golf Club, "A Unique Nine-Hole Course," appears by a sandy single-lane track. After passing over a large cattle grate, the road winds about 500 yards through a working farm towards the sea. The Isle of Arran looms in the distance across the Firth. On a sunny day it seems impossibly close. From the small parking area, a sandy path snakes through the whins to a small dark green building. A pavilion is defined as "a decorative building used as a shelter in a park or large garden." This term, used by the 1911 *Scotsman* journalist, seems appropriate for Bute.

On approach to the clubhouse, the first-time visitor could be in for a shock. A motion detector activates an automated announcement of *"WELCOME TO BUTE GOLF CLUB"* in a deep, somewhat menacing, voice. The phantom speaker goes on to give instructions for using the honesty box. The first time I visited in 2021, the sudden unexpected declaration nearly scared me to death.

Scale is critical in architecture. The size of this tiny Victorian treasure, its simple lines reminiscent of Corrie, is perfect for the links of Bute. On one side, beautifully weathered wooden lockers silently tell the story of decades of friendship and camaraderie. This patina can only be earned through time. Modern craftsmen cannot recreate it. A small meeting room makes up the other half of the simple floor plan, the perfect place for a hot drink to recover from cold wind and rain off the Firth of Clyde.

This is a simple, proud structure. It complements the remote, natural links on which it has stood for over 110 years. For visitors seeing it for the first time, it is like discovering an unexpected treasure in the wilderness. It is hard to quantify what makes a building fit ideally on its site, but the Bute clubhouse captures these elusive qualities.

On my day at Bute, I went around twice and only saw three other golfers—a grandfather with two small children who were teeing off the 1st hole as I finished the 9th. I sat on a bench at the clubhouse and watched them play the first two holes, the children sprinting between short shots that rolled along the ground. The peaks of Arran were obscured by clouds. The Firth of Clyde shimmered, silver and blue, in the intermittent rays of sunlight. The only sound was the wind and crashing of waves in the distance, broken up by shrieks of delight from the tiny running golfers. I got up and walked to my car, careful not to set off the motion detector on the old clubhouse and break the reverie.

## − − − ISLE OF SEIL − − −

Eight miles south of Oban, at Kilninver, the B844 intersects the main west coast road. The single-lane country track winds through a rocky, rolling landscape dotted with sheep. Around every sharp bend, the landscape looks like one set of natural golf holes after another, just waiting for someone to place a flag in the ground. After a few glorious miles, the steep, arched structure of the Clachan Bridge comes into view. This marvel of engineering and Scottish masons was completed in 1793 and still carries vehicles over the narrow channel of the Clachan Sound to the Isle of Seil. The bridge is more commonly known—with an element of dry Scottish humor—as The Bridge Over the Atlantic.

The village of Balvicar, home of the nine-hole Isle of Seil Golf Club, is located three miles past the bridge. It consists of a group of small cottages along Balvicar Bay and a post office. Green fees can be paid in the general store/post office, which is located at the start of the narrow lane that leads to the golf course. I visited Isle of Seil Golf Club for the first time in August 2021. When I stopped at the small store to get a bottle of Orange Lucozade and pay my green fee, I told the friendly cashier/postmaster that I only had time for nine holes. "Well," she replied, "the green fee is the same for nine holes or all day. It's £15." This critical lack of distinction says a lot about why golf is so great in Scotland.

The road from the post office hugs the small cottages on the left and higher open land on the right. When the narrow lane ends abruptly, a sharp right turn suddenly reveals the bright turquoise green of the Isle of Seil clubhouse. A sign nailed to a power pole in the gravel car park reads:

POLITE NOTICE. GOLF CLUB.

Isle of Seil Golf Club was formed in 1995, thoroughly modern by any standard. It took several years of planning and fundraising for the club to have their own golf course. Suitable land was eventually found on Winterton Farm, which was thought to be the site of a long-abandoned golf course from the early 1900s. The first club captain, Donald Campbell, laid out the wonderful nine holes—which wind among ancient rock formations and the tidal inlets of Balvicar Bay. Large rabbits—the size of small dogs—wreak havoc on the greens, but that is part of the charm. A group of members take care of the course. The smooth turf has a wonderful, bouncy, machair-like quality. This type of golf is not for people expecting Muirfield-like conditions. It is a place for those that believe golf in its most elemental form is worth seeking out. The land is for use by the community as much as it is for golf. You are as likely to encounter people out walking their dogs as you are other golfers.

A clubhouse, only in the most generous definition of the word, was erected in 2008. As is the case with everything at Isle of Seil, the members pitched in to convert an old wind damaged garden shed—replacing the roof and one wall. The remarkable painting scheme was decided on by consensus of the members. It is a tiny structure, no more than 200 square feet. Even the most well-traveled golfer is likely to smile at the sight of this festive wee shed. This building proclaims that Isle of Seil Golf Club is a place for fun. Near the 1st tee, a St. Andrew's Cross flies proudly next to several benches, all painted the same bright neon green.

The single ten-by-twenty-foot room is jammed, in an impressively organized fashion, with club notices, sign-up sheets, photos and a plastic bin of old golf balls on sale for 20p each. An old church pew sits along one wall. If you neglected to pay your nominal green fee at the post office, there are honesty box envelopes and a register to dutifully record your visit. This small interior is breathtaking in its organized simplicity. This is the home of people who love the game for all the right reasons. It is the essence of golf distilled into one room.

### — — — TRAIGH — — —

A bothy is a traditional Scottish structure. The word is derived from the Gaelic word *bothan*, meaning a simple shelter, usually left unlocked, for hikers to use free of charge in remote areas of the Highlands. The term is also often used to describe the traditional Scottish croft house, a small, rectangular masonry structure with fireplaces located at each gable end. In these uncomplicated structures, the ground floor consisted of an open living area with windows and a kitchen. Two sleeping areas were situated over the lower rooms. Crofters worked the land, raising livestock, usually paying an annual rent for their small cottage to an often-absentee laird.

There has been a golf course on the farmland of Traigh (a Gaelic word meaning beach) since the early 1900s. It is located seven miles south of the port town of Mallaig. The original course was a part of the farm. Greens were "fenced off" with railway sleepers to keep off the cows and sheep. Holes crisscrossed wildly. A rudimentary shed served as the clubhouse for a few local members.

When the owner of the land, Jack Shaw-Stewart, retired from his job in Edinburgh in 1989 he decided to expand and renovate the old layout. He worked with John Salvesen, a former captain of The Royal & Ancient Golf Club of St Andrews, to create an almost entirely new course. Salvesen's brilliant design work resulted in a modern masterpiece of Scottish golf. The new holes take full advantage of the property and the stunning views across the beach to the Small Isles of Rum, Eigg, and Muck. As part of this complete transformation, Shaw-Stewart made plans to erect a clubhouse near the coast road and the new 1st hole—a brilliant uphill 136-yard par three to a shelf-like green cut into the massive hill. The location of the new building proved to be another brilliant move. The view of the 1st tee at Traigh with the nearby small, white clubhouse is now one of the most recognizable in golf—to a certain type of golfer.

Initially, Shaw-Stewart considered providing a simple prefabricated wooden building to greet golfers at his new course. After finding one he thought was suitable, he took his wife Vora to see it. The manufacturer informed them the model in question had "blown away" in a recent storm. Obviously, this would not be suitable for a completely exposed location near the beach on the west coast of Scotland. The couple decided to engage a local architect to assist with developing plans for a permanent structure.

Two initial pavilion-like designs were rejected out of hand by the Shaw-Stewarts. Vora was insistent that the architect should design a "proper building" in keeping with the scale of traditional Highland crofts. She felt the clubhouse should be based on the historical Scottish "but and ben" style croft layout, which consisted of two rooms with a chimney at each end. The thoughtful client was also adamant that the building should be painted white. A reluctant architect provided revised plans, which Mrs. Shaw-Stewart felt were still out of proportion. To prove her point, she measured the ruins of an old two room croft located in the woods near the golf course and then insisted the architect incorporate these exact measurements into the design. Like the brilliant Scottish stonemasons of old, her instincts proved to be correct. The planning department of the Highland Regional Council enthusiastically approved the revised plans. In 1993, the new clubhouse opened. It has now become a well-known and beloved symbol of remote Scottish golf.

The large open interior room is filled with natural light from windows on three sides. A comfortable built-in bench with soft cushions runs the length of one wall. On the opposite side of the room, a tea and coffee maker are neatly situated next to a rack of candy bars and crisps. There is a desk for the club secretary to accept green fees and watch over it all. It is hard to imagine a more intimate, welcoming space for visiting golfers.

Artist David Shaw-Stewart, David and Vora's son, has depicted the serene coastal scene in many of his paintings. He marvels that the small white clubhouse has become so iconic, but credits that to his mother's insistence on incorporating traditional proportions and colors. The modest, but carefully planned, building has helped Traigh Golf Club grow and welcome more visitors each year. It shows how a thoughtfully designed building, however small, can enhance the experience of playing golf. If you are ever fortunate enough to make it to the remote links of Traigh, you will be greeted by a structure that looks as if it has been sitting near Traigh Beach for 250 years. In many ways, thanks to Vora Shaw-Stewart, it has.

After an early spring 2024 round in the mist and rain at Corrie, one of our playing partners, Greenskeeper Ewan McKinnon, unlocked the tiny old Victorian clubhouse so we could sit and dry out for a few minutes. Ancient silver trophies sat gleaming on top of the burnished, time worn, wood lockers, near the cathedral ceiling, the lovely work of some long-gone joiner. Nobody spoke for a few minutes. The happy feelings of a friendly match, one that was in doubt to the last shot, were enough for the moment—along with the wonderful, strangely refreshing, feeling of tiredness that comes from walking the hills of an ancient Scottish glen with three good friends. It was enough to simply rest and be thankful that places like this still exist.

# 4

## Brora

# Serene and Majestic

"Granting all this, however, James's golf was entirely magnificent. He dominated the tournament from beginning to end, serene, majestic, and inevitable."
—Bernard Darwin, *James Braid* (1952)

Why do we love golf? Maybe it's the feeling of walking alone on a crisp, windy morning, in a gently flowing landscape by the sea. Maybe it's feeling the simple joy of spending four hours with a good friend. Maybe it is the feeling of executing just the right shot under the pressure of a closely contested match. In truth, it is a combination of all these things and more. There are certain places in the game, like Brora, that have an additional element—a spiritual feeling. A walk around the links of Brora makes me happy that I have lived my life as a golfer.

This perception of spirituality is palpable at Brora. The natural elements of grass, wind and water create a natural sanctuary, providing a few hours of welcome escape from the stress of everyday life. The charms of Brora are subtle, yet they can inhabit a space in our golfing mind for a lifetime.

Crofting rights are sacred in Scotland. In 1897, Brora Golf Club had nine holes, and the members were looking to expand the links to a full 18, which were designed by the legendary Scotsman James Braid. The remainder of the adjacent wonderfully rolling linksland was controlled by cattle farmers, who were part of a Common Grazing arrangement, which allowed golfers to share this precious ground with often skeptical crofters. In 1916, the Duke of Sutherland asked the Land Court to ban horses from the property, but the farmers retained the privilege to graze cows and sheep on the links. Electrified wire fences keep the animals off the always perfectly maintained greens.

Remarkably, this arrangement continues to this day—though the club is currently seeking to end it. Golfers still share, as of now, this ethereal landscape with roaming sheep and Highland cows. What is viewed—understandably for local members—as a detriment, is seen by many visitors as a part of the unique charm of playing golf at Brora. The club had long seemed to accept its coexistence with the farmers. Most members now desire, as is their right, to have a course that is more easily maintained. The ever-present cattle can wreak havoc on the course conditions. Over time, the experience of playing Braid's masterpiece amidst massive Highland cows became synonymous with a visit to Brora. If those days are over, as they appear to be, I will enjoy the memories. It will in no way lessen the greatness of this serene links.

My first visit to Brora was a happy accident, as so many of my best experiences in Scotland have been over the years. In 1994, my knowledge of golf in the wilds of the Scottish north was largely limited to Herbert Warren Wind's seminal 1964 story in *The New Yorker*, "North to the Links of Dornoch," and Michael Bamberger's 1993 book *To The Linksland*, both of which feature the legendary Royal Dornoch Golf Club. Neither writer mentions Brora, not even in passing. My father and I had traveled north to play Dornoch on our first trip to Scotland, largely because of these two American writers. After a couple of days on that wonderful links, we had a day with nothing planned. During breakfast our host at Highfield House in Dornoch suggested that we head twenty minutes north to play a place called Brora. Before we could even agree to his suggestion, he had called the pro shop and booked us a time.

"There is a club competition going off at 9, but they will let you out just in front if you get there in time. Off you go," said our friendly landlord.

After a quick exchange in the pro shop, we hurried to the 1st tee, high above the lovely beach, to find a group of about thirty members waiting for the competition to start. The 297-yard first hole at Brora is a classic James Braid opener, designed to ease the tight golfer into the round. Braid first visited the course in 1910 and spent a day walking around with a map of the layout, making notes and revisions as he went, before catching the train back south. He returned a few weeks later and made some suggestions to refine his plan. For this service of two days on site, he was paid a fee of £25. The course today remains virtually unchanged from the Great Man's original 1910 plan. Brora is part of the James Braid Highland Golf Trail, which also includes nearby Golspie, Boat of Garten, Inverness, Muir of Ord, Fortrose & Rosemarkie, and Reay. Braid laid out more than 400 golf courses, and some of his best designs are concentrated in the Scottish Highlands.

As you stand on the 1st tee at Brora, the green appears for all the world to sit on a rise directly in front of you. It looks like it is about 300 yards in the distance. On that long ago July morning we played naively away, into the wide fairway, in the direction of that green. After promising members not to hold up the monthly medal, we strode off ignorantly and happily to find our tee shots. My dad hit what appeared to be a great shot right at the green in front of us. As I was preparing to play my approach in the same direction, I was interrupted by a shout from one of the members proceeding quickly—running in fact—down the fairway. "No, no, that's the 17th green! The 1st is over there," he exclaimed, gesturing at almost a 90-degree angle to the right. He kindly offered us a course guide, which proved invaluable in directing us around the links. The 1st green, situated perfectly in the dunes near the beach, was only a wedge shot away.

Fast forward 28 years, and I was back at Brora again, alone this time. On the drive up from Hopeman and the lovely course there, I stopped to spend a few hours walking around the ancient battlefield at Culloden. A low, gray mist was hanging over the moor when I arrived. It is hard to imagine the horrors that occurred in such a beautiful place. A Scottish Highlander's memory is long—and for good reason. It is important to remember the lessons of history, lest we forget them. If you are fortunate enough to ever visit this unique part of the world, take the time to experience a few things other than golf.

This time around, I booked a 9 a.m. tee time, arriving early to have tea and a roll, with sausage and egg, in the wonderful upstairs bar. The upper floor of the curiously modern clubhouse has a stunning view of the par-three 18th and the North Sea beyond. Malcolm Murray, the head professional, greeted me warmly in his tremendous golf shop.

"Are you out by yourself today? We are booked solid starting at 8, but you can get out ahead of everyone if you want to go on now," he said kindly.

My breakfast roll and tea would have to wait. What solo golfer has ever refused the promise of a wide-open course?

There is a precious and rare type of silence to be found in the early morning on a seaside links in Scotland. The sound of the waves quietly breaking on the beach, the wind—not too strong at this early hour—blowing through the native grasses, the sound of clubs clicking together in a carried golf bag and wandering sheep baying their constant chorus all combine to create a natural orchestra. If you are ever first to go off the tee, alone at Brora, it is an experience to be treasured. The walk between shots offers a clarity to the mind that is different from almost anything else. The world becomes clearer, and its possibilities seem limitless. A solitary stroll around the links of Brora has a restorative power for the body and soul.

Braid believed that the natural landscape should dictate the layout of a golf course. This theory is perfected at Brora, which sits elegantly in the terrain as if it has been there forever. Like Elie, where Braid learned to play the game, the holes flow naturally from one to another, evoking a satisfying sensation of constant movement. I have played Brora several times over the years, but I still get a sense of nervous excitement every time I walk down that 1st fairway.

Brora is a traditional out-and-back links. On my most recent visit, the wind was straight behind going out, which meant, of course, that it would be the exact opposite coming in. The 2nd hole, called Bents, continues a wonderful opening stretch of pure links holes. Once again, the tee is situated above the lovely beach. I looked back to make sure no other groups had reached the 1st fairway yet, wanting to sit for a moment and take in the scene. A good drive will leave the opportunity to play a traditional low, running shot to another green that is in exactly the spot it needs to be. At Brora, almost every shot offers the traditional, creative choices afforded by true links golf.

Three other holes on the opening nine stand out to me. The 325-yard 4th, White Post, might be considered easy by critics like Tom Doak, but I love it. A drive down the right-hand side will leave the best angle for another running pitch to a beautiful green marked by a tall, white directional post. Two massive Highland cows stood guard by the 4th green on this solitary morning. They looked friendly, but a good Scottish friend had once warned me that "a cow is not your friend, Jim." I kept a respectful distance.

The 6th and the 9th, both par threes, have occupied a permanent place in my mind over the years. The 178-yard 6th, called Witch, breaks the direction of the "out" routing, turning left at 90 degrees. It requires a precise shot to an elegantly bunkered green. The 146-yard 9th, the Sea Hole, is one I have often thought about over the years. It plays towards the sea and beach beyond, with the green—at least in the past—almost always surrounded by sheep. On this day, one of the many wandering sheep walked in front of the tee and stood there looking at me, completely unconcerned by my presence. The view from this tee is one of the most memorable in golf.

On the 10th tee, the course turns towards home. The holes on the inward nine are a bit further from the sea, and a few of them stand out. The 125-yard 13th hole, called Snake, is a sublime, short par three. An impossibly winding burn makes its way between the tee and green—and out to the sea. The green is guarded by five deep sand pits. Once again, a group of massive Highland cows grazed by the burn in front of the tee, oblivious to my presence. This hole is a work of art.

The character of the inward side is just slightly, almost imperceptibly, different. It is no less enjoyable. The 16th and 17th are a great pair of holes. The 16th, a 345-yard par four called Plateau, forces us to play the most uphill approach shot of the entire day to a green situated on what must be the highest point of the course. Once you reach the top of the hill, the entire world of Brora reveals itself. It is one of the sacred spots in golf. Take the time to sit on the bench for a moment and enjoy the scene. The tee shot on Tarbatness, the 438-yard 17th, is my favorite one on the course. From an elevated tee, two large bent-covered mounds in the fairway must be avoided, leaving a longish approach into a welcoming green with the sea beyond. Like its designer, Brora is serene and majestic. It is inevitable that you will have fun.

Brora ends on a difficult uphill 201-yard par three, perfect for viewing by members in the upstairs bar. Thanks to the kind gesture by Malcolm Murray, I got around the course quickly. In about three hours I had walked back into his shop to find him slipping on a caddie bib.

"How did you get on, Jim?" he asked. "I'm going out to caddie. We don't have enough members around today." The head pro at Brora was going out for a loop with a group of Americans on their first trip to the course. This is the perfect demonstration of the sincere welcome shown to visitors at Brora.

It was still early when I finished my round. I had nothing planned for the afternoon. A decades old friend of mine in the U.S., Jammy Erwin, loves fly fishing. I wanted to bring him back some local flies from the various areas of Scotland. This search was sort of a minor subplot to my trip and was almost as much fun as the golf. While having a drink in the Brora clubhouse bar, I messaged a friend at Golspie, Alasdair MacDougall, to ask if there were any good fly-fishing shops in the area. He responded almost immediately: "Aye, I think there is a wee shop just up the road in Helmsdale that might suit you."

Helmsdale, which I had once driven past quickly on a trip to Durness and Reay, was a kaleidoscopic twenty-minute drive north on the A9. The blinding hillsides of yellow gorse and fields of golden rapeseed, with multiple shades of green, gave way to impossibly blue vistas of the North Sea. One of the major challenges of driving in Scotland is not to let yourself be too distracted by the natural beauty. It can be overwhelming at times, especially in the Highlands.

The small village sits next to the River Helmsdale, one of the most renowned salmon fishing rivers in the world, and between the surrounding mountains and the sea. It is like something out of your most vivid dreams of Scotland. You could almost reach out and touch the gorse covered hillsides towering over the town. It was around noon when I walked into a small café called Thyme & Plaice, on the town's lovely main street, to order some lunch. It was still a bit early, so I had the place to myself. The chef and the café owner were more than happy to talk to their lone customer. They knew Alasdair, of course, and we had a long discussion about the joys of both Brora and Golspie.

After a nice lunch, I asked the friendly restaurant owner if she knew of a fly-fishing shop in town. She smiled and said, "Yes, I do. Just look out the window, straight across the street. Yvonne has a lovely wee shop called Glencoast. She will sort you out."

I thanked my hosts in the café for their kindness and walked across the street to search for fishing lures. Yvonne seemed to know just what I was looking for. She helped me select several local, brightly colored flies and carefully placed them in a small box that I knew my old friend would love.

"I'm not a fly fisherman. I just play golf," I told her.

"I am cursed to do both," she said with a laugh. "I usually play at our wee course here in town."

As I was walking out the door, she said, "stop at the bridge and take a wee photo of the flies with the river in the background to send to your friend." I took her advice. The bright blue Helmsdale River sparkled in the afternoon sun.

Thinking I would drive back to the Golspie clubhouse and take in the late afternoon views of that wonderful links, I headed out of town. Almost immediately, I saw a sign for "Golf Road." I could not resist the urge to see what was there. The narrow track followed the river for about a mile through a lovely glen, when suddenly I came upon the course, Helmsdale, looming in front of me like a Harry Rountree watercolor painting come to life. It took me about two seconds to decide that I had to play.

The car park and the tidy, small clubhouse were both empty. There was an honesty box by the door. Grabbing a half set of hickory clubs from the back seat of my rental car, I walked out into yet another undiscovered wonderland of Scottish golf. Hole after hole at Helmsdale was pure fun, perfect for the hickory clubs. There were benches located on many of the nine teeing grounds, so I took my time and enjoyed being alone in this stunning glen on a bluebird day. Nobody else was on the course. The hillsides of vibrant, blooming gorse screamed the eternal promise of spring.

In thirty years of visiting this ancient and exceptional country, I have never experienced a scene quite like it. After holing out for par on the downhill 9th, with the green situated right by the clubhouse and the 1st tee, I left a note of thanks in the honesty box to go along with the modest fee. The morning round at Brora had given me more energy than I had any right to expect.

Early the next morning I left the Golspie Inn, where I had stayed for several days. The sky was clear once again, and I could not resist the short drive back to Brora for one last look. The car park was empty. I walked down to that 1st tee above the beach and paid my silent respects to Braid's masterpiece. After a few moments of reflection, listening to the natural symphony of Brora, I went back to the car. Boat of Garten, another Braid tour de force, awaited me in the afternoon. A part of my heart will always be in the Highlands.

**5**

# Carradale

## The Pudding Bowl

"We get an odd one misusing the honesty box, rarely, but right enough, we usually get them."
—Carradale Greenskeeper Robert Strang, in Tom Morton's *Hell's Golfer*

There is an inherent natural wildness to golf on the Kintyre peninsula, a long, narrow strip of land tenuously attached to the Scottish mainland by a thin slice of terrain at the village of Tarbert. The picturesque town sits at the juncture of East and West Loch Tarbert—its lovely harbor acting as the unofficial gateway to a mythical golfing Nirvana. To a certain type of golfer, the names of the Kintyre links are spoken in hushed tones of reverence—Machrihanish, Dunaverty, Machrihanish Dunes. While not as well-known as its more celebrated neighbors, there is another course that deserves a place in this illustrious pantheon. The nine holes of Carradale Golf Club float above the Kilbrannan Sound like a Caledonian dream.

My dad allowed me to plan our entire 18-day itinerary on our first trip to Scotland, the only stipulation being that we must play the Old Course and Carnoustie. Other than that, he said we could go wherever I wanted—and I wanted to go to Machrihanish. The drive from Glasgow Airport was magical. We left the city, crossing over the Clyde at the Erskine Bridge and then onto the A82 which hugs the western shore of spectacular Loch Lomond. After a sharp turn west on the A83 at an old country hotel, there was a long stretch along glorious Loch Fyne down to Lochgilphead and finally into Kintyre. The great English golf writer Pat Ward-Thomas eloquently described the same trip in 1960:

> "We left the Clyde towards evening on a golden Sunday and it was wonderful to see the traffic lessening as we came to Inverary, to know that there were still 80 miles to go and that the workaday world was receding fast. I shall not forget the magic of that drive along Loch Fyne, all gleaming silent peace, and the marvel of the sunshine dying over West Tarbert Loch, gold and purple, silver and black."

We stopped for a late lunch in Tarbert. Like Ward-Thomas, I will never forget the sun reflecting off the harbor when we walked out of the small café'. My dad and I sat on a bench for a few minutes looking at the multi-colored boats. To our left were the ruins of a castle on the hill above town. It all seemed unreal to a boy from Alabama. An hour later we arrived in Machrihanish for several unforgettable days. I discovered Dunaverty on that same trip, but never even heard the name Carradale mentioned during my nightly Tennent's-fueled discussions in the old Machrihanish clubhouse bar. The place made such an impression on me that I immediately inquired about joining the club, which I did with the help of David Baxter, our wonderful host at nearby Ardell House.

A few years later I became a member at nearby Dunaverty, a place I had grown to love even more than mythical Machrihanish. I felt at home on the Kintyre peninsula. After all the time I have spent over the years in this corner of the world, I feel that love even more now. As joyful as the visits are, it has become increasingly painful to leave. More than a few tears have been shed leaving Southend, along the road to Stewarton, on my way to Arran or the Glasgow airport.

A second trip to Kintyre came in 1997. After several days in the area—which included the best 95 ever shot in a gale in the Jimmy Kerr Open at Machrihanish—we left early one morning to catch the ferry to Arran. Against my better judgment, I took the B842, the eastern road from Campbeltown to the Claonaig ferry landing. After about 40 minutes of driving on the most winding and harrowing road I had ever seen, the village of Carradale appeared. A small sign for the golf club caught my attention. With just a few minutes to spare for the 10 o'clock sailing, I turned down a narrow road to find a small white clubhouse next to the 1st tee. The tidy, square building was unlocked. Inside, placed neatly next to an honesty box, were a stack of simple white scorecards with a map of the course. I took one and walked out onto the first tee. The 1st hole intrigued me—a straight uphill blind par three—as did the 9th green which sat invitingly to the right of the tee.

Time is precious for a visiting golfer in Scotland. Arran and its promise of discovery awaited that day. Our boat from Lochranza would arrive soon. Carradale would have to wait.

The Kilbrannan Sound was like a sheet of polished steel that

morning—the low rumbling engine of the approaching ship offering the only interruption to the preternatural silence. On the top deck of the ferry, I looked back to the headlands of Port Righ while considering what I missed. The modest scorecard was placed in my photo album of that trip—and later at home I often studied its simple diagram of the nine-hole layout. Despite several visits to Kintyre in the intervening years, this passing stop was my only experience at Carradale until much later, on a sublime morning in May.

As my dad had done for me so many years before, I took my son Jake to Scotland in the spring of 2019. It was his first trip. My parameters were simple. The itinerary would include Dunaverty, Shiskine and Machrihanish. If the schedule worked out, I would take him to Cruden Bay and Prestwick, too. Other than that, I told him we could go wherever he wanted. I like to leave some elements of Scottish travel to the random nature of chance. When you leave yourself open to the unknown, the result can often be extraordinary.

Jake surprised me by saying that he wanted to play courses like Covesea and Carradale, not the normal options for the first-time visitor. I could not have been happier with this. We drove around the east coast for several days, often stopping wherever the mood took us. We played Elie in Fife, then Fraserburgh and Cullen as we went north to the links of Covesea. The 18 day trip was to end in Kintyre and on the Isle of Arran. On a bright, clear morning, we left the Ardshiel Hotel in Campbeltown and drove along that same serpentine coastal road to play golf at Carradale.

For weeks prior to our visit, I had corresponded with the then club secretary at Carradale, Rhona Elder. Our plans changed frequently as we progressed around Scotland. She was always cheerful and accommodating when I revised the date of our visit. Even though the remote nine-hole course would likely be empty on a May weekday morning, the formality of prior arrangements is something I respect and enjoy. There was a single car in the small gravel car park when we arrived for our 9 a.m. tee time. The small clubhouse had been expanded a bit since 1997. The secretary appeared to formally greet us.

"Mr. Hartsell? Good morning. Welcome to Carradale. You have the course all to yourselves just now. Robert, our greenskeeper, is about if you have any questions."

I had secretly hoped we would meet Robert Strang. He has been the sole caretaker of this headland paradise for more than 30 years. His name had appeared in *Hell's Golfer* and a few other things I had read. Some of my best conversations about golf have been with Scottish greenskeepers.

As we started to walk through a small gate to the nearby 1st tee, Ms. Elder spoke again, in a strikingly serious tone.

"One more thing, Mr. Hartsell. The committee has met and afforded you the honor of playing off the medal tees today. Off you go. Enjoy your game."

As we warmed up to start our round, she drove away. I was moved by this unexpected privilege, even without the knowledge that the medal tees at Carradale offer some of the most spectacular views to be found. At Anstruther, we had been chastised by the greenskeeper for playing off the medal tees. Now we had permission to play them all.

It was a beautiful morning, and I was about to play a course in Kintyre, with my son, for the first time. I found that 22 years proved to be far too long a delay for golf at Carradale.

Carradale Golf Club was founded in 1906. A story in the July 14th edition of the Campbeltown Courier described the scene that day:

> Golf Course at Carradale
> NEW GROUND OPENED FOR PLAY
>
> Carradale has taken a decided step forward in recognising the claims of the golfer in its arrangements for attracting the summer visitor. Golf enters much into the thoughts of the modern holiday-maker, and the place claims his patronage cannot long afford to deny him facilities for the indulgence of the game. The

credit of originating the Carradale course belongs to the laird, Austin MacKenzie, Esq., while Major W. M. Hall of Torrisdale also took a keen interest in the new venture. Mr. MacKenzie had the ground marked off under his own direction, and afterwards it was gone over by Mr. Munro, the Machrihanish professional. The course is a nine-hole one. It is situated between Airds and Port Righ, and embraces two fields on the home farm and the ground known as Castle Park.

The article goes on to describe the opening day ceremony in detail. Mr. MacKenzie, Esq., hit the inaugural tee shot and declared the course open for play before giving way to the local minister and committee member, Rev. G.S. MacLeod. The minister thanked the laird for the use of his land and praised his skill in assisting with the course layout. Like Tarbert and Dunaverty just down the road, the course was laid out by locals who just wanted a place to play. No earth was moved during construction. There was no reason to. Nature provided the perfect playing field.

The reverend ended his impromptu speech by stating boldly that "the course has a beauty and scenery and bracing air not to be surpassed in all of Scotland" and "enough risks and hazards to command all a golfer's skills." These statements still hold true more than 115 years later.

On a cold, windy morning in April 2023, I left my cottage at Dunaverty Rock, in a rented Skoda Octavia, with my friend Todd Schuster, aka Tron Carter of No Laying Up, in the passenger seat. The brilliant No Laying Up cinematographer, Matt Golden, sat in the back seat, recording our conversation for a documentary about my book, *When Revelation Comes*. We'd take our time driving up to Oban, stopping for nine holes at Carradale.

After a quick visit to Muneroy Tea Room in Southend to say goodbye to owner Frances Hill, and to grab a scone and tea, we were on the road. A right turn at the Glen Scotia distillery in Campbeltown put us on the same long and winding road I had first driven in 1997 and a few times since. The B842 climbs up quickly to the hills above town, past beautiful old mansions from the halcyon days of the whisky industry. As we passed the holy island of Davaar, with sheep cascading down the verdant green slopes to the sea, it became clear that the road had been improved greatly. The carriageway was still narrow and twisting by any normal standards, but it had been widened a bit in some of the more dangerous spots. The conversation that Matt recorded was the excited banter of golfers anticipating a special day.

The car park was empty, and the clubhouse was unlocked when we arrived at the course. I hope the world never reaches the point where doors must be locked at Carradale. There was nothing but vast blue above us. The yellow, green and purple landscape sparkled in the morning sun. Cows grazed idly in the fields adjacent to the 9th fairway. I went inside to place our £15 green fee in the honesty box. The excitement from my friend was palpable as we walked through the narrow wooden gate to the first tee. The opening par three, blind, sheer and vertical, is an exciting start, but it is at the top of the hill when Carradale explodes across your senses.

"You get to the top of that hill on the 1st and it's like, wow! It's like something out of a fairytale. You kind of get hit in the face with those views but then you realize that this is a real golf course, too. That 2nd hole is brilliant—down the hill and over the stone wall back up to that almost infinity type green. It sort of sets the tone for the round," marvels Todd Schuster.

From the elevated 2nd tee, Kilbrannan Sound—and Arran beyond—appeared in front of us like a panorama of dream golf. The next few holes are wonderful. It is all there at Carradale. There are blind shots, weird green sites benched into the sides of massive hills, and hidden tees with vistas that seem endless. On the 4th tee, you can see Shiskine in the far distance, across the water.

The mountains of Arran rise dramatically, almost defiantly. We stood for a minute in respectful silence and took it all in. Shiskine was our destination in a few days, so this preview was like an exciting film trailer. Every hole was good, perfectly foreshadowing a great one—Pudding Bowl, the par-four 6th at Carradale.

From the 5th green, itself a wonder of golf architecture carved into the side of a steep hill, it is a long walk back to the medal tee on Pudding Bowl. There is a narrow, uphill footpath through rabbit holes, heather, gorse, fescue, and all forms of natural Scottish vegetation. When you stand on that tee, it is like being on top of the world. It is subjective to say that a hole is unique. I can only say that I have never played another one exactly like the 6th at Carradale.

Ken Brown, a Scot, five times European Ryder Cup player, and noted golf commentator, discovered Carradale while on holiday in the area in May 2019, just a few days before my visit with Jake.

"Our cottage was only 50 yards from the 3rd tee, so naturally I went to investigate, and I loved what I saw! I bumped into Robert the head greenskeeper and enjoyed chatting with him about how he maintained the course," Brown recalls.

Pudding Bowl is the well-traveled former tour professional's favorite hole on the course.

"The tee box was elevated and the views it gave you of the hole and the sea behind you were just incredible. My favorite part of the hole was how the small green was set into the side of the hill and how that affected your strategy off the tee."

The hole is only 306 yards. A mere choked-down three-wood for professionals, but the perfect length for normal golfers. From the medal tee, the fairway appears to sit somewhat perpendicular to the line of play—although it is really angled sharply to the right. The tee shot must carry a corner of Port Righ Bay and the beach. Crucially, the decision rests on how much to cut off over the beach and rough, bog-like, tall fescue covered ground. The farther left you go, the better the angle you will have into the bizarre, laugh-out-loud perfect green. The tradeoff is that the carry for your drive gets increasingly longer.

Following the lovely walk back to the medal tee, Schuster had the honor—but was trailing in our game, 1 down. We were competitors in a hotly contested match, but openly discussed the intriguing challenge in front of us. A long hitter, he went for the heroic line towards the green. The wind was coming into the tee. It was a perfect strike. He laughed as he recalled the moment.

"That was one of the best shots I hit on the whole trip! It was kind of like picking your poison. You sort of have to decide how far left you want to go. You were playing great in the match, so I sort of had to go for it. That tee box is as spectacular as it gets. It's the first picture I show people when I'm telling them about Carradale."

I played safely to the right and found the fairway. The angle into the green was not ideal, but my ball was in play. We never found Schuster's ball. The match ultimately went to 2-up in my favor.

It is a challenge to adequately describe the 6th green at Carradale. It is sort of a punchbowl, but it is not quite that. I suppose that is why it's called Pudding Bowl.

"That green site is probably the best one I played last year, along with a couple at Dunaverty and Machrihanish. There is that little fence around the green. It's totally nuts. It is truly one of those holes where you are thinking 'this can't possibly exist.' You would never build something like that today. Honestly, it doesn't look like something you would build 100 years ago—and I mean that in a good way," says Schuster.

A wire fence on the fringe keeps livestock from trampling the grass. This sheltered part of the course is still used as grazing land at certain times of the year. There is a feeling of isolation from the other holes when standing on the curiously elongated, cloistered green. An aggressive approach shot can be played off the slopes on three sides, funneling the ball onto the narrow putting surface which is cut into the top of a rocky mound. Bluebells, heather, and gorse frame the scene—exploding in bursts of violet, deep purple and yellow, depending on the season. Any shot that comes up short will funnel down the steep bank at the tight opening to the wonderfully bizarre green complex. Key to the hole's strategic design is the green: angled in such a way that it only opens itself to golfers that have taken the bold line from the tee.

"The Pudding Bowl can either hurt you or help you, depending on what kind of bounce you get. The way it sits there in the land is just so cool. It's so unique to be on a nine-hole course and feel so secluded from the rest of the property. Carradale is one of my favorite places I've ever been," says the well-traveled Schuster. The thoughtful No Laying Up member has played many of the world's most well-known and celebrated courses, places that most golfers only dream of playing like Royal Melbourne and Cypress Point. His display of sheer joy while walking around a remote, £25 for a day ticket, nine-hole course on the Kilbrannan Sound is a reminder that golf in its simplest form can be as transcendent as even the most celebrated venues.

Jake lives about an hour from us now. We get to play golf occasionally, usually with my other son Jonathan. I do not see either of them as much as I would like. Children grow up, we hope and pray as parents, and live their own special lives. I have several photos of Jake from that 2019 trip on my office wall. They are from Dunaverty, Carradale, Shiskine, Covesea and Anstruther, the smaller, lesser-known courses that we both love so much. We mostly stay in touch these days through random, usually humorous, short text messages about music and sports—*"Richard and Linda Thompson are underrated"* or *"Patrick Cantlay is a frozen statue"* or *"I can't stand watching Purdue play basketball."*

In early 2023, Jake's work schedule finally allowed him to consider returning to Scotland with me. We started planning another trip together. Late one night I was in bed and a text message popped up on my phone: *"The 6th at Carradale is my favorite hole in golf."*

# 6

## Corrie

# The Enchanted Glen

We'll all meet next year
I can safely foretell
In the wee public bar
Of the Corrie Hotel

Oh, the Corrie Hotel
The Corrie Hotel!
In the heart of a village
Where I long to dwell

The tales of the regulars
Are too tall to tell
In the wee public bar
Of the Corrie Hotel
—from *The Corrie Hotel Song*,
performed by Kenny Ritchie

It is a typical August Tuesday night in the Corrie Hotel bar on the Isle of Arran. Three dogs sit calmly at their masters' feet, an English Setter, a golden retriever, a West Highland Terrier, oblivious to the loud revelry surrounding them. A large Scottish man, Kenny Ritchie of Corrie, wearing a green tartan kilt turns from the bar with a pint of Tennent's and suddenly launches into song, in a lovely, deep baritone. When he reaches the chorus, Corrie Hotel regulars join the anthem—*"Oh, the Corrie Hotel, the Corrie Hotel!"* The enthusiasm of the makeshift choir is impressive and contagious. The problems of the outside world are easily forgotten in this remote country inn.

Seen through the ancient bay windows, Sannox Bay is smooth and shimmering in the dull grey twilight. The echoes of the impromptu *ceilidh* were fading as I took my pint down to the bay. An otter pops its head up quickly and surveys the scene for a moment. The old granite and limestone hotel—all of 15 rooms—is glowing with a bright yellow light from inside the lively bar. The Corrie sits at the bend in the road just as it did in 1850, when carriages and horses were the only mode of transport. A few patrons quietly enjoy a drink and a takeaway fish supper in the bayside garden. An occasional car creeps by slowly along the A841, the passengers curious to see what they are missing. A typical summer night in the Corrie Hotel.

About a mile and a half past the hotel, in the tiny village of Sannox, lies the nine holes of Corrie Golf Club. Located in the shadows of the mighty peaks of Goatfell and Cir Mhor, it was laid out in Glen Sannox by locals in 1892 to give workers from the nearby barytes mines a place for exercise in the fresh, open air. The May 19, 1892, edition of *The Glasgow Herald* gives this account of the club's genesis:

CORRIE GOLF CLUB

To the attractions of this popular seaside resort there has recently been added a golf course. A club has been formed and a managing committee appointed, consisting mainly of visitors who resort regularly to Corrie. The Rev. Mr. Muirhead, of Corrie Church, has been appointed captain, and the secretary is Mr. H. Moxon Cook, artist, who during his lengthened professional sojourns at Corrie has done much to make the place attractive.

The "links" farm is very suitable golfing ground near the mouth of Glen Sannox, upon the farm of Mr. McAllister, the course, a nine-hole one, lying up the hollow between the Sannox Burn and the farm-house. The five outward holes reach up the Glen to the footbridge, where the steeper ascent of the hill begins and turf gives place to heather and granite; the sixth hole is across the opening of the Glen to the shearing-house, which serves as a "bunker" for the unwary driver; the three home holes are played down the slope.

The turf is in excellent condition, and the course affords good scope for full drives, as well as for the brassey and the iron. The trees, the ditch, the "bog" and the bracken supply abundant hazards, without their being "sporting" or converting a holiday recreation into a toil. The scenic environment, which often adds greatly to the attractions of golf, is of the grandest on Corrie course. Going out the golfer is looking right into the heart of the Arran mountains, and having turned home he is looking down the Firth, with Bute, the Cumbraes, and the Ayrshire coast beyond.

On a 167-square-mile island with six other fun, unique golf courses, Corrie stands out as an ideal example of the type of exhilarating, affordable golf that can still be found throughout Scotland. Visitors to the island can purchase the Arran Golf Pass for a mere £140—the cost of playing six holes at legendary Royal Troon, only 17 miles across the Firth of Clyde from Whiting Bay Golf Club. With this pass—golf's version of Wonka's mythical Golden Ticket—visiting golfers can play rounds at Shiskine (12 holes), Brodick, Whiting Bay, Lamlash, Lochranza (11 holes!) and *twice* at nine-hole Machrie Bay and Corrie. There cannot be a greater value to be found in this increasingly expensive game.

If you decide against the golf pass, a day ticket at Corrie is only

£25. You can play as much golf as you want after 5 p.m. for the imposing sum of £15. The sun sets on Glen Sannox around 10 pm in July and August. A golfer could manage four trips around this compact 1,915-yard layout and still get back to the hotel in time for a late bar meal. In an era of increasing greed and arrogance in golf, Corrie reminds us of what made this game so special 130 years ago. A brisk walk in a beautiful, natural landscape with good friends, while hitting a ball into a hole, is still the soul of this ancient pursuit.

In April 2023, I convinced my friend Todd Schuster (aka Tron Carter) of the U.S. golf media outlet No Laying Up to visit Arran. The demands on the group's time—and the number of places they are asked to visit—are astronomical. Despite the implied pressure associated with such a strong recommendation, I was confident in my endorsement. The resulting three days of golf with old Scottish friends—and a new friend, Corrie greenkeeper Ewan McKinnon—was even better than I had anticipated. We spent each evening in the Corrie Hotel bar—recounting the good shots and laughing about the bad ones—over a long meal, ending with a flight of Arran Ice Cream and a cheese plate with the local oak smoked cheddar. None of us wanted those nights to end.

The course golfers find in Glen Sannox is largely unchanged from the *Glasgow Herald's* description. A walk on the lush turf of Corrie, with the mighty peaks of Arran rising above you like the mountains of Tolkien's Mordor, is a pure thrill. You will come off the 9th green and likely want to go straight back to the first tee—although a brief visit to Fran's Tearoom would be wise. There you can pay your green fee for another round and stop for an apple crumble with a restorative pot of tea. There is no reason to rush. Life moves at a slower pace on Arran. The Corrie Hotel bar—and wonderful conversation with happy people—will be waiting for you.

Breakfast in Scotland is a holy sacrament. The formality of it is wonderful. It is best to enjoy it and not rush the experience. One morning, during my initial visit to the Corrie Hotel several years ago, I was the first resident to come downstairs to eat. A friendly white-haired gentleman immediately appeared from the kitchen and took my order of smoked salmon and scrambled eggs.

"You can make your own toast," the man said, as he gestured towards an industrial size toaster across the room.

As he went about busily arranging the room for the morning crowd, we started a pleasant conversation. I must have arrived a few minutes too early, but he did not seem to mind. There was a beautiful English Setter sitting quietly on a sofa just outside the breakfast room, which I later learned belonged to my host, Tony Burrin. He seemed genuinely interested in my plans for the day. Finally, a few more lodgers appeared. I finished my toast and headed off for golf. It was my only morning in the Corrie Hotel on that trip. My brief interaction with Tony left me in a pleasant mood as I started up "The String" at Brodick and over the mountains to Blackwaterfoot and the glories of Shiskine Golf and Tennis Club.

When I returned to Corrie the next summer, Tony and I continued our conversation as if it were simply the next morning and not a full year later. This time I was around the hotel for several breakfast conversations. In addition to being the daytime chef, I learned that he had another all-consuming passion. "My second book was just published," I mentioned between bites of toast and raspberry jam. Tony responded excitedly, "I run the Wee Bookshop just down the road. You must come by after your golf. I'll be there until 5."

After 21 holes of golf on Arran—nine at Corrie and twelve at Shiskine—I made the drive back over The String to the eastern shore. A detour at Tarrnacraig took me through a single-lane farm track. A large ewe and two small lambs skipped across the road, oblivious to my oncoming vehicle. When I entered the Corrie Wee Bookshop late in the afternoon, Lottie the English Setter was resting on a pillow by the door. She raised her head slightly and glanced at me, then quickly resumed her rest, unphased by my presence. The proprietor was working on a laptop next to an ancient-looking cash register. The scene was like the idyllic dream of a small bookshop. Books were displayed from floor to ceiling—*The Summer Isles* by Philip Marsden, *The Arran Malt* by Neil Wilson, *The Coffin Roads* by Ian Bradley.

No more than 250 square feet total, it is a miracle of efficiency and organization. The books are mostly on topics related to the history, wildlife, and natural environment of Arran—but there is also a nice amount of modern Scottish fiction. When Tony learned that *When Revelation Comes* included a chapter on Arran, he graciously offered to stock a few copies. This is a greater honor than if my book was displayed in the front window of The Strand in downtown New York City.

Tony Burrin moved to Arran from London in 2016 after a lengthy career in the restaurant business. Working at the hotel gives him a chance to meet new people, something that he loves. He can often be found giving visitors advice on how to enjoy their precious time on the island. Books are a special passion:

"I love talking and selling books to folks who really love the island. First time visitors are often completely infatuated within an hour of getting off the ferry at Brodick. I love seeing kids and young people in the shop who love books and reading. It beats the Kindle and the bloody computer any day!"

Burrin is currently working on a book of his own, *The Arran Almanac—A Guide to All Things Arran.* The Corrie Wee Bookshop is open most afternoons.

Just beyond the challenging turn off the B880 in Sannox into the car park, the small green Victorian jewel that serves as the Corrie clubhouse sits next to Fran's Tea Room. The tiny building was erected in 1897 and remains almost unchanged in the intervening 125 years. Beautifully weathered dark wood lockers and ancient trophies line the interior. If the tearoom is not open, an honesty box is located on the porch to accept your modest green fee. A few steps beyond that, just through the gate, and you are on the first tee a Corrie—a lovely, sheltered 127-yarder that plays directly over the 9th green. It is at the 2nd tee, however, that the

majesty of Corrie and Glen Sannox reveals itself in earnest.

On a sunny day, this view up the glen is majestic. A lovely oak sits directly in front of the 2nd green, which can be accessed by playing off a mound to the right of the green, all to avoid the venerable tree—which appears to be the same size in the earliest known photos of Corrie. A large "2" is spray-painted in white on the trunk, almost certainly there to reassure visiting golfers that they are not hallucinating. The nearby Sannox Burn flows musically around large rocks as you study the remarkable scene. Tall, mighty peaks of Arran explode from the ground into the sky like computer generated images. It feels as if you could simply reach out and touch them. If your tee shot has been played successfully off the mound on the 134-yard hole, the ball will funnel onto the punchbowl green. It is a wild, fun shot, like many at Corrie.

Starting at the 3rd tee, just as in 1892, the walk into the enchanted glen begins in earnest. The landscape has not changed much over the centuries. The peak of Cir Mhor is an almost overwhelming presence. In 1912's *Isle of Arran* by Reverend Charles Hall, he beautifully described his first view of Glen Sannox:

> "So soon as the head rises above the ridge a superb surprise view is seen: Glen Sannox is stretched before us, flanked by mountains; its stream from this elevation appears like a white meandering streak, and beyond is the blue of the Sound of Bute, backed by the island from which it has its name. Above, to the left, the towering cliffs of Cir Mhor frown upon us, and on the other band a knife-edge ridge rises to North Goatfell."

This perfect little uphill par four—which plays across both the 7th and 8th holes—ends at a green which rises vertically, almost comically, out of the lovely turf. The first time I saw it, I fell hopelessly in love with Corrie. To stand on the 3rd green at Corrie, with Cir Mhor rising above into the endless azure sky, is an experience to be treasured.

The man who takes care of this enchanted glen is Ewan McKinnon. He was born in Sannox, a village of about 25 people. Golf was one of his only ways to amuse himself as a boy.

"Well, I was the only person under the age of 50 in Sannox, so playing golf at Corrie was how I passed my time, "he recalls with a laugh.

At age 16, Ewan started working part-time during the summer on the small Corrie greenkeeping crew. Experience with his parents' landscaping company and his love of nature made him well suited for the challenging work of a golf course superintendent. "I really enjoyed working the summers with Pablo, the greenskeeper at the time. I learned a lot from him," he says. This apprenticeship came while he was developing into an excellent golfer—one of the best on Arran.

A thoughtful and soft-spoken man, Ewan's game eventually became good enough to compete several times in the Scottish Amateur. He made it through the qualifying and to the match play rounds at Western Gailes in 2011. "I was playing my best golf at that time. In the third round, I came up against Scott Borrowman, who is now one of the pros at Stirling. He was not even playing that well and he just hammered me 7&6. It's just a different sport at that level. It was humiliating," McKinnon recalls. In 2015, he made two holes in one in the same nine-hole round at Corrie—on the 5th and the 8th. The odds of this occurring are about 67 million to one.

Despite his humble nature, Ewan remains one of the finest golfers on Arran. He has a powerful, flowing swing and still plays as much as his work allows. In a recent round with his good friend Greg McCrae of Brodick, Jake, and myself, he started the round with a 2, following it up with eight consecutive 3s—for a 26. It is as flawless a round of golf as I have ever witnessed in person. The holes he did not birdie were all tap-in pars. Corrie, a collection of five par threes, and four par fours, plays to a surprisingly challenging par of 31.

In October 2017, he became the full-time greenskeeper at his home course. It is clearly a labor of love for McKinnon. Greg McCrae, a course regular, gives him much of the credit for the current emergence of Corrie in golf circles:

> "It's just a testament to what Ewan's done with the place the last few years, because for me growing up, Corrie was just a small, wee nine-hole golf course. You were nearly classing it as a kind of pitch and putt. Most of the visitors coming to Arran wouldn't go near Corrie. People are now coming and giving Corrie a chance and leaving there going, "Wow!" It just generates more visitors. Corrie is now, I would say, the second-choice golf course for anybody coming to Arran to play on holiday. Shiskine, yes, you've always got that. Everyone hears about Shiskine. But if anyone asks, where should I play? Corrie is now the second choice. And back 10 years ago, it would have been the seventh choice out of our seven courses on Arran. It makes a big difference having a greenkeeper that can play the game of golf. That helped hugely on the golf course, just the way Ewan sets it up. He has made the course so playable and enjoyable—and obviously, the views sell it as well."

McKinnon takes on the myriad challenges of being a solitary caretaker—time, equipment budget, leatherjackets, marauding red deer, weather—with characteristic positivity. He would love to have Corrie play as hard and fast as its more famous neighbor, Shiskine. "The weather from the Atlantic comes straight over the top of Shiskine, hits the mountains and drops straight down on Corrie and Brodick. You'll see Stewart (the greenskeeper) at Shiskine begging for rain and Corrie will be green and lush," he says.

Despite all the challenges, he maintains Corrie like a living work of art—which in many ways it is.

Around the same time as he started to learn the art of golf course maintenance, Ewan became a volunteer for Arran Mountain Rescue. The Arran Mountain Rescue Team is called out as many as 50 times during the summer. He has been a member of this volunteer group for more than 20 years. The squad gets calls for twisted ankles, broken legs, stranded walkers, all manner of accidents that can happen in a hiker's paradise like Arran. He once participated in the rescue of a paraglider who crashed into the side of a cliff and was trapped by his parachute. A Navy helicopter had to be called in to assist with the operation. It is dangerous, but rewarding, work. The years he has spent with the rescue squad say a lot about his character and commitment. He has the look of a man who climbs mountains. "These guys all do this voluntarily. They just drop everything and go whenever help is needed," McCrae marvels.

At the 4th hole, we enter the rockier area of the glen. Now there are patches of purple heather and the occasional splash of Open Championship yellow gorse. This lovely par three plays from a pulpit tee down to a beautifully sited, almost hidden, green close to the rushing waters of the burn. On the 5th, one of Ewan's dual ace holes, the climb is straight back up the hill that we just came down. It is an almost vertical, blind par three. Now we are reaching the heights of this wonderful, madly routed, layout. The sixth, called Shearing House, is a testing par four, and possibly the "best" hole at Corrie. It plays across, and up, the lovely hillside, to another hilariously good green benched into the side of the hill. The sheep shearing house from 1892 is gone now, but this hole remains unchanged.

There are occasions that make you "give thanks for your life as a golfer," as the Scottish writer Angus MacVicar once so eloquently wrote. The 7th tee at Corrie represents one of those rare moments, like the 11th green at Askernish or the 9th tee at Cruden Bay. Most of us are ready for a brief respite at this point in the round. The climb has been sharp over the last two holes. Behind the 7th tee—taking full advantage of the view across the Firth of Clyde to West Kilbride and Ardrossan on the mainland—sits one of the world's great golf course benches. Created from a massive bog oak tree trunk, it is the work of local wood sculptor and Corrie member, Marvin Elliot. His art studio in the heart of the village is a wild menagerie of carvings of seals, dolphins, dogs, and mysterious, shadowy figures.

"Marvin is an incredible sculptor but a bit of a tortured golfer," says Ewan McKinnon. "He plays almost every day. He keeps his clubs hidden behind the buggy shed, cycles over from Corrie and plays five or six holes every afternoon. I know of at least one occasion that he threw his clubs in the bin only to retrieve them later that day."

After a few moments of silent reflection on Marvin's bench, it is time to let a shot fly downhill from the highlands of Corrie to the 7th green on the lower level of the glen. Our drive is played across both the 6th and 3rd fairways, of course. With the Firth of

Clyde shimmering in the distance, this is surely one of the most enjoyable shots we will ever play. A good strike will provide a chance for birdie, though it is a curiously difficult hole. This is the apex of fun, sporting golf.

The par-three 8th plays back into the secluded, wooded corner where we started from. It also serves to get us to the 9th, a short par four that is McKinnon's favorite hole on the course. "It's a great match play hole. You can try to play a draw with a long iron or wood over the wee burn to the green or lay up with a wedge or nine-iron over into the 2nd fairway," he says. The green sits just where it is meant to be, at the base of a slope leading up to a primordial forest of oaks, larch and Scots pine.

Arran is a living history museum of traditional Scottish golf. It is a natural feast for our senses. Corrie gives us a view of the world that artificial intelligence can never replicate. It is the same as it was in 1909 for Rev. Charles Hall:

> "The best days on which to traverse Arran's glens and mountains are when a moderate breeze blows from the north-west and the sun shines after some days of rain. Then the peaks and ridges stand out sharply in a scintillating atmosphere, and the glens are seen in every detail. But this is seeing Arran in a summer mood, he alone knows the island who tramps it in all weathers and in all seasons. Let Goatfell be climbed when snow glistens on its ridges, and a snell blast from the north is blowing; traverse Rosa and Sannox during a fierce south-wester, soaked to the skin by torrential rains, and when the tracks are all running burns, and each footfall is accompanied by a splash. Ascent the hills when the mists are low upon them, and every step has to be calculated to make sure; when indeed, it is easy to be lost, and one realizes what it means to be alone. It is in doing such things that one gets to appreciate the soul of a country, and to understand it in the making of a soul of a people."

After our spirited match with Todd and Greg, Ewan opened the clubhouse for a minute of post round respite. The names of the ancient champions of Corrie were all around us, engraved on the old silver medals and trophies. There is something comforting about history and respect for the past—for all the golfers who have walked this enchanted glen through time. We talked, but in low and almost reverential tones. It was the talk of tired, content golfers happy to be out of the cold, windy mist.

In a quiet moment, the experienced world traveler Todd Schuster leaned over to me and whispered, "I can't believe this place."

This island will get under your skin. As you toil away at work in the throes of winter, with the thought of playing golf a distant prospect, your subconscious mind will plot ways to make your return to Arran and Corrie. It is so much more than golf. It is the eloquent greenskeeper Ewan McKinnon, who maintains this ancient golfing ground as only a boy who grew up in Sannox can. It is Tony Burrin, who left the tumult of London looking for a quieter life filled with pleasant conversation, books, and red squirrels. It is the brilliant wood carver Marvin Elliot, who is tortured by the game, but cannot resist its hold on his soul. It is the Corrie Hotel, where people sing in the bar on a Tuesday night just because they can. It is Corrie Golf Club in Glen Sannox—a place where reality can surpass even the wildest fantasy.

# INTERLUDE

## Sandy Watson of Southend

"The road to Southend, right down at the southerly tip of Kintyre, hence the name, snaked through fragrant farmland, until suddenly there was the sea, a wide sweep of silver sand, a hotel, the Argyll Arms, some houses amid the fertile fields, and a bizarre concrete pseudo-castle, also a hotel."
—Tom Morton, from *Hell's Golfer* (1994)

The rain was blowing sideways at Dunaverty Rock—a stony peninsula that was the site of the last significant Kintyre stronghold of Clan MacDonald in 1647. The dark gray skies and howling wind scouring the bay were not a good omen for my first ever round with the Dunaverty Heidbangers, a raucous group of members who have played in all conditions every Wednesday since 1999. Despite the ominous weather, I made the short drive over to the clubhouse. The weather can change quickly in Kintyre.

As I unloaded my clubs, I met Linda Brannigan in the small car park. Her husband Bill had organized the now infamous group into a weekly Stableford competition more than 25 years ago. I asked Linda if she thought the boys would venture out in this weather,

"I don't know, but the women would," she said with a laugh.

I had started towards the clubhouse when she added, with obvious emotion in her voice, "I brought a scrapbook Bill kept of the Heidbangers. I hope you'll have time to look at it. He would be so pleased you are playing today."

The Dunaverty clubhouse is like the den of a large family home during a holiday gathering. It could be Christmas or New Year's Day, but the holiday is golf—and it is a daily occurrence. The lively conversation on this dark and forbidding morning was only interrupted when someone had a bite of one of Moyra Patterson's rolls, with egg and Lorne sausage, or a sip of tea. One of the men holding court—in front a large glass display cabinet filled with Empire biscuits, apple crumbles and sponge cakes—laughed as he saw the lone American, water dripping off his expensive, useless waterproofs, approach the raucous gathering.

"This is when the course plays the best, Jim! Oh, you'll really see how she plays today. This is true golf!", he proclaimed loudly to the entire group.

"Are you going out?", asked one of the men seated at the crowded breakfast tables.

"Ach, noooooo, not me! No way in Hell I'd go out in this mess!"

As laughter rattled the rain-streaked windows, an elegant white-haired gentleman, with a mischievous glint in his eyes and a bemused smile, sat in the middle of it all. At 86-years-old, Sandy Watson had seen and heard it all in his 72 years as a full member of Dunaverty Golf Club on the rocky shores of the Mull of Kintyre. There is some debate in the club as to whether 89-year-old Scottish golf legend Belle Robertson or Sandy has been a full member for longer. There is not any debate about who is the oldest playing member.

Sandy Watson first started playing golf at Dunaverty—where his father Duncan was the club steward and professional for 50 years—at around age 4. "I had a wee club my dad had cut down for me. We'd go out and hit balls around the first two or three holes like kids do," he recalls with remarkable clarity.

His father taught him the basics, a good grip and proper etiquette, but like many of us he learned to play golf by playing all the time, as only golf obsessed kids can do. Angus MacVicar, the poet-laureate of Southend, wrote this about the Watsons in his 1974 memoir, *Heather in My Ears:*

> "Dunaverty Golf Club has over a hundred male members and about 50 ladies. Having played the course regularly for almost 50 years, I know every bunker and rabbit-scrape in its tortuous 4,614 yards. The standard scratch score is 63. Oddly enough, however, the professional record, held by Eric Brown, is 65. The amateur record is 62. This was set recently by Sandy Watson, a son of Old Duncan, the club steward. I think golf, like singing, must be hereditary. Old Duncan, at the age of 77, can still go around in his age. Two years ago he celebrated his golden wedding by handing in a score of 75."

As the great Angus MacVicar attested, Sandy learned to play very well, eventually becoming club champion at Dunaverty multiple times. He also inherited his father's golfing longevity, beating his age virtually every round he plays—which is at least three times a week, often more. "I don't even have to arrange games. They are arranged for me," he says with a smile and almost a sense of wonder. The elderly are treated with respect and honor in Scotland. They are valued for their wisdom and life experiences. Staff in the wonderful clubhouse restaurant, The Putt Stop, look after him as if he were their own grandfather. Whenever I've had a question about the history of Dunaverty over the years, the response has invariably been, "Ask Sandy. He'll know the answer." A conversation with Sandy Watson is an experience to cherish. He lives about 50 yards—walking distance—from the clubhouse. He rides his bicycle everywhere else he needs to go. He has lived in Southend his entire life

Sandy remembers things that would now otherwise be lost to the mists of time. Playing amongst grazing sheep and cows on both sides of Conieglen Water, before the club purchased the property east of the river from a local farmer. Playing golf with Angus MacVicar, "a fine partner and a good player, though he got a wee bit upset with himself at times." The 14th green being the old 1st green, when members played from town on an opening tee just outside the Argyll Hotel. The green on the 4th as part of a long par five that played from around the current 1st tee. The downstairs bar in the now ghostly, abandoned Keil Hotel—which haunts a round at Dunaverty like an ancient clan stronghold. The old, corrugated metal clubhouse, which sat roughly between the warm-up net and the current car park—a place where his beloved dad held court for so many years. He remembers all these things.

The rain had temporarily abated enough that the entire group went out to the 1st tee, just outside the large clubhouse windows, to watch each three-ball game go off. A variety of jeers cut through the keening wind, which was now blowing harder, if anything. A nice drive was applauded. A weak pop-up was almost blown back into the assembled group's faces, eliciting a round of good-natured jibes. Our group was the last off, so David MacBrayne and I were spared the certain ridicule when an 86-year-old man easily outdrove the both of us, straight into the invisible wall of wind. "I'm nae getting the length now, Jim," said Sandy—with a total lack of irony—as the three of us strode off the tee. "My swing is so much shorter than it used to be." All this coming from a man that sometimes walks five or six rounds of golf a week and still occasionally wins club competitions.

Sandy credits golf with his long life and good health, both mentally and physically. "Being out on the golf course is good for you. It helps keep you fit. It helps keep your mind clear," he says. There cannot be a better example of this simple, beautiful theorem than this man. It is his maxim for life.

He has made many aces at Dunaverty over the years—multiple times on the 4th, 7th, and just a few months prior, at the long, difficult 14th, one of the toughest holes on the course. He counts the 7th—a 175-yard par three called "St Andrew" as his favorite hole on the course. "Yes, yes, the 7th. It's just a nice short hole in the dunes. You must land the ball in just the right spot," he says in a lovely, lilting, sing-song voice.

Watson makes a textbook par on the vastly underrated, difficult par-four 1st, sinking a curling five-foot putt with an ancient blade putter. "I used to play a nice high shot into this green," he says wistfully, "now it's strictly a run-up for me." The putter looks like the famous Calamity Jane that Bobby Jones used to win the 1927 Open at St Andrews. Almost on cue, the cold rain starts to pelt down and across like angry bees swarming a hive. We huddled together on the 2nd tee waiting for the green to clear. I asked Sandy about the old putter. "It was my dad's. It's the only one I've ever used." Sure enough, the ancient blade is stamped with the words:

D. Watson
Southend

We struggled along through to the 5th, David and I laughing at the futility of it all. The conditions were hellish, but Watson continued to hit one elegant, low-running shot after another. On the

5th fairway, we see some of the Heidbangers slowly making their way back to the clubhouse. The best £350 waterproofs are useless in this kind of weather. David MacBrayne had finally reached his limit as well.

"Right, let's play to the 17th green from the 6th tee and in. That's enough of this," said the longtime Dunaverty greens convener. I never heard Sandy complain once about the brutal conditions. As bad as it was, it was wonderful to play those last two holes with the two of them.

I was playing golf with two wonderful men at my favorite place on earth, but I had never been more relieved to have a round shortened to seven holes. (Note: The 6th tee to the 17th green is a wonderful cross-country hole should you ever have the chance to play it.) My thoughts drifted to a large bowl of Moyra's carrot and coriander soup. The temperature had dropped at least 10 degrees in what seemed like seconds.

We all managed to par the 18th, largely because there was a 35-mph gale at our backs. Dutifully removing our useless waterproof bucket hats and shaking hands, Sandy looked me straight in the eyes and said, "Now we know each other properly. We've played golf together."

True wisdom cannot be faked. It is earned through the experience of living life in the best way you can. No one can deny that Sandy Watson has lived his life the right way. When he speaks, it is with an inherent, simple, wisdom.

The next evening, the club held a junior golf event. Parents and energetic, smiling children crowded the clubhouse, waiting for the festivities to start. It was a perfect late afternoon on the Mull of Kintyre. The hurricane of the previous day was a distant memory. Moyra's dessert case must have run out of empire biscuits within 15 minutes. The full staff had come in on their day off to serve soup, toasties and hot drinks to the happy crowd. I saw Sandy sitting by himself at the window, with a bowl of soup. "Back for more?" I asked with a laugh. "I wouldn't want to miss this tonight, Jim." The twinkle in his eyes was even brighter, if that is possible. He invited me to join him at his table, as he has done every time I have ever talked to him here.

The format was simple and perfect. Each child was to be paired with an adult for a seven-hole alternate shot tournament, on the very loop we had played in a raging hoolie the day before. I watched Sandy tee off with 9-year-old Lyle Ramsay, a child over 75 years his junior. This young man had no idea that he was playing golf with a legend of the game. Something tells me his parents may tell him when he is a bit older. Either way, I am sure it is an evening he will remember for the rest of his life. This is how the wonderful game of golf is passed on between generations. This is how it has always been in Scotland.

After the prizegiving, which was a large chocolate Easter egg for the first three places, I said goodbye to Sandy and complimented him once again on his wonderful play. His response was typically self-effacing:

"I'm just lucky to be here."

The true face of golf is not Rory McIlroy, Scottie Scheffler or some other factory-produced, absurdly wealthy, golf professional. It is 86-year-old Sandy Watson of Southend, Scotland, who lives 50 yards from the 1st tee at Dunaverty Golf Club.

Southend.  Dunaverty
Valentines Series

# 7

## Covesea

# A Hidden World
# on the Moray Firth

"Earth, ocean, air, beloved brotherhood!"
—Percy Bysshe Shelley, "Alastor" (1816)

On a beautiful spring day in 2019, my son and I made a spur of the moment decision to make a bold (or foolish) attempt to play nine more holes of golf—on a day that had already included 36 holes at Fraserburgh and Cullen. Jake had seen a photo or two of Covesea online, but that was all we knew about the course.

"It looks great, Dad. We have to try to get there and play."

When my son has an instinct about a place, he is always right.

Our new friend, George Clark, eyed us skeptically in the Cullen Links car park when I mentioned this idea.

"I haven't really heard of Covesea. It's getting a bit late in the day," he said, as we loaded our clubs for the 40-minute drive to Lossiemouth. Driving a bit too fast up the A98 and playing that final nine holes before dark proved to be one of the best decisions that we made that trip.

The entry drive to Covesea Links, a nine-hole course near Lossiemouth, is quintessentially Scottish. The single-track gravel road off the B9040 winds unassumingly through gorse for about half a mile, before you crest a ridge and the links suddenly is revealed before your eyes. It is a somewhat rare thing for Scotland—a relatively new course that only opened for play in 2010.

The sun was already low in the western sky as we pulled into the small car park near the caravan from which the proprietors Angela and Andy Burnett run the course. Angela came out to greet us, the only golfers going out at 7 p.m., the beginning of golden hour.

"Have you had your dinner yet?" she asked.

"No, we are going to stop in Lossiemouth after the round."

"Oh, I better book you a table. 8:30 is usually the last service. Let me call now."

Before we even got our clubs out of the car, Angela had secured us a reservation for 8:45 at a local restaurant. The Scottish people seem to offer small kindnesses as a matter of course. Imagine a golf course operator in America calling to book reservations for two golfers who had just driven up out of nowhere—it would be unheard of.

"You'll be able to get around in 90 minutes at the most," said our host.

Covesea Links is easily walkable, with tees smartly placed only a few paces from each previous green, like most of the great Scottish courses. Our green fee that day was £10. The Burnetts reluctantly increased this to £15 in late 2019. Angela seemed to feel almost guilty about the escalation at the time:

> "This was our first price rise in 10 years. It has always been a vision of Andy's to have a "pay and play" quality golf course at a price that means it is inclusive to all. A place where a scratch golfer can play along with a family member or friend who are beginners, with no pressure."

These are admirable goals and the true essence of Scottish golf. I confess that I love everything about Covesea Links. A round today costs £25, but that is still a great value.

The course was, and continues to be, a labor of love for Andy Burnett. He has a background in golf course maintenance and construction, having previously built the widely admired Dragon's Tooth Golf Club (now known much less colorfully as Woodlands Glencoe) at Ballachulish. When the Burnetts acquired this seaside property in 2004, it had been used mainly as sheep grazing land. Andy built the course over a period of six years, with some assistance from his employees at times, and he still serves as the main greenkeeper for the links. The course is a family run affair, as Angela explains:

> "Andy attends mainly to Covesea Links and Miles, our youngest son, is now also a greenkeeper and works here and at another course that Greenstaff Services (Burnett's company) have been hired to do greenkeeping and specialist works. We do have other family members who help when needed, including our eldest son Andy Jr. and Cousin Joe. Most of the work at Covesea Links is done by Andy—hand watering till 1 a.m., out hand cutting at 6:30 a.m. in the height of the golf season."

The par 31 course plays wonderfully firm and fast, as a seaside links should. In addition to Burnett's obvious greenkeeping skills, his routing is brilliant. Greens are sited just where they should be—in a natural punchbowl, on top of a dune or hidden behind a giant red rock "sea stack" like those at Cullen. Tees are perfectly placed. The views from the 6th and 9th tees at Covesea rank with any course in Scotland—or in the world for that matter.

In a lifetime of playing golf, the ethereal golden quality of the low sunlight illuminating the gorse-covered rocky hills on this late May afternoon surpassed anything I had ever seen. It is sometimes reckless to make definitive statements like this, but I feel it is warranted in this case. Jake and I walked around the entire nine holes, making comments like "Wow. Look at that. Unbelievable." It was a "golden hour" to exceed even the wildest dreams of Percy Bysshe Shelley.

I love all nine holes at Covesea, but there are four standouts for me:

- The 402-yard, par-four 4th hole, with its tee next to the Moray Firth. The fairway looked like the firth itself in the late afternoon sun, with each mound and undulation highlighted by the surreal golden light.
- The wee 90-yard, par-three 5th plays straight uphill to a green cut into the top of a dune. The view from this green, with the sea and the Covesea Skerries Lighthouse in the distance, like the view up Glen Sannox at Corrie, is sublime.
- The completely blind 135-yard, par-three 7th, which plays over a massive red rock to a green situated perfectly at the base of the hills beyond, is reminiscent of the wonderful 13th at Cullen. There is nothing more fun than the anticipation after a well-struck shot on a blind par three.
- Finally, another Faberge, jewel box par three, like the 10th at Aberfoyle, the 104-yard 9th. The tee is benched into the side of the gorse-covered cliff and plays to green with a backdrop of the entire majestic links and the firth beyond. It is one of the best views you will ever have on a golf course.

As the only golfers out on the links, we went around the course quickly—despite our phones never being put away. The light was just too exceptional, suffusing the rocky landscape in an ethereal glow. We finished at 8:30, just as Angela had predicted. The brilliant golden light was starting to fade as she came out to say goodbye, the family dog by her side. "Thank you for coming by. I hope you enjoyed our wee course," she said as we loaded up the car to rush to our dinner reservation. A hot bowl of Cullen Skink and a pint was going to be most welcome after walking 45 holes of golf, starting at Fraserburgh, then Cullen, and ending in this hidden cove.

Angela Burnett clearly loves running a golf course with her husband and seems amazed that people now come from the ends of the earth to visit Covesea. "The people we have met from all over the world who are still in touch, and support us from afar, mean everything. We are living the dream," she says.

Since our first visit in 2019, Andy Burnett has continued to work on improving his course—a new back tee was installed on the 9th, and several green sites have been modified. I have no doubt that it has only made this small wonder of the golf world even more enjoyable.

Michael MacAllan, the head professional at nearby historic Nairn Golf Club, discovered Covesea Links a few years ago. It has become his refuge from the challenges of day-to-day life, says the thoughtful Scot:

> "The course awakens your senses and challenges your judgement from the moment you climb up onto the 1st tee. It is 2,000 odd yards of relentless golfing fun. It has a bit of everything—beautiful wildly contoured greens, marram grass galore, breathtaking elevation changes and more than a little bit of the Scottish blind shots. It is the most charming golf course I know. There isn't anywhere else in the golfing world like it. There is so much to treasure about the beautiful little golf course; and about Andy and Angela who pour their hearts and souls into the place every day. The thing I love most about Covesea is the lack of pretense, the absence of ego. I love Covesea."

Thankfully there are people like Angela and Andy Burnett who just want to share their dream of affordable Scottish links golf with the world. If you ever make it to that part of Scotland, I suggest trying to time your visit for around 7 p.m. on a clear day in May. Be prepared to keep your phone out. Covesea is beautiful.

4th Tee Cruden Bay Golf Course.

# 8

## Cruden Bay

# Amongst the Tumultuous and Mighty Dunes

"To take first the philosopher, what kind of course shall we assign to him?"
—H.N. Wethered and T. Simpson,
*The Architectural Side of Golf*

Much has changed since my first trip to Cruden Bay in 1994. The course was then in largely uncharted territory for visiting foreign golfers, who ventured north of St. Andrews and Carnoustie mainly to visit Royal Dornoch. There was a thrilling sense of adventure and discovery in finding an unknown links, at least for an American. The welcome extended to visitors in the small, utilitarian white clubhouse was warm and sincere. The course we found all those years ago was wild and fun.

Those things have not changed in the intervening years. While Cruden Bay ceased to be unknown a long time ago, as tour buses filled with golfers will attest, the course and the treatment of visitors remain the same. If anything, the course is even better than it was 30 years ago.

Change, when it comes, does not proceed with haste in Scotland. That is not criticism, it is just the way it is. When a country is so old, history is revered, and change is sometimes viewed skeptically. It can take years for a golf club to debate over even a minor revision to a course, or for the government to update old infrastructure. The drive up from St. Andrews was not an easy one in 1994. Today it is made with relative ease, given the addition of the A90 bypass of Aberdeen. This stretch of motorway has cut at least 30 minutes off the drive time from years ago. Not that I recommend bypassing the famed granite city of Aberdeen, but time can be precious on Scottish golf trips.

You may feel a slight pang of regret heading north on the A90 at Stonehaven, thereby bypassing the wonderful Stonehaven Golf Club and historic Royal Aberdeen, but sometimes difficult choices must be made. If your one dream golf trip to Scotland is to be based in St. Andrews, a day at Cruden Bay is worth the extra effort.

The visual revelation of the linksland of Cruden Bay is a thrill, no matter how many times you may have been there. Walking from the car park, around the striking modern clubhouse, (a major change since 1994) you are confronted by a panorama of dunes and linksland that is unique in golf. The towering and mysterious ruins of Slains Castle are visible in the distance, enhancing this glorious tableau of massive sandhills in an almost theatrical way. It is one of the most stunning reveals of a golf course that can be experienced. It is unforgettable.

It is thought that golf was played on these grounds as early as 1791. The genesis of the current links dates to 1894 when the Great North of Scotland Railway Company commissioned the course and hotel to promote railway tourism. Old Tom Morris himself provided the initial routing. Cruden Bay Golf Club was founded soon thereafter in 1900. The current course layout dates to 1926 and is the work of renowned English architect Tom Simpson. A major, and inspired, revision to the links occurred a few years ago—and it was one of the best surprises of the day.

On a beautiful, windy, spring morning, Neil Murray, the head pro, greeted us warmly in his wonderful golf shop. It is one of the best in Scotland, filled with all kinds of merchandise. He asked if I had played the course before.

"Yes, several times, but it's been almost 20 years."

"Well, you will find it much the same as you remember, except for the 9th and 10th. We built a new 9th hole a few years back and relocated the tee on the 10th."

It was not a busy morning, so we talked about my memories of the course as I looked around the well-stocked shop. Jake had gone outside to warm up. I mentioned that it was my son's first trip to Cruden Bay, and it happened to be his birthday. It was an off-hand comment.

A starter, another change since my last visit, was waiting for us by the 1st tee. The original late-Victorian era clubhouse sits nearby, now lovingly converted to a museum of Cruden Bay's golf history. Since I had played the course before, we were asked if another American could join us—it was his first visit. You rarely meet unpleasant people on a golf course, so I was happy to be a tour guide. The man introduced himself as Chris, from California.

Despite the almost 20-year gap in my experience, it was surprisingly easy to remember the correct lines. My dad and I played Cruden Bay a lot in those early years. On almost every hole, each shot has an optimal line that is not easily discernable. One of the most joyous aspects of links golf is the strategy of where to land the ball on the ground.  This is especially true at Cruden Bay.

The opening tee shot should favor the left side and must avoid a bunker, but it is not a stressful start to the round. The approach to the 2nd, to a raised plateau green, is one of the best on the course. At the 3rd, a reachable par four, you start to enter the wild heart of the links. At 268 yards, the blind tee shot must land between dunes on both sides, which will funnel the ball down to the perfectly located green. A well struck ball may result in an eagle chance, but an offline shot can result in a double bogey or worse. It is a great hole.

It would be natural to expect a letdown after the pure joy of the 3rd, but it only gets better. The 4th hole is one of my favorites. The tee is set behind the 3rd green, with the fishing village of Port Erroll and the river—called the Water of Cruden—to the left. At 196 yards from the medal tees, it plays slightly uphill over a valley between the dunes and the river. The sheltered green sits perfectly among the sandhills, with a constant wind blowing through the grass covered dunes providing a natural, almost hypnotic, chorus.

Beginning with the tee shot at the 5th, the course enters into duneland that rivals the great Irish courses. The next four holes are routed masterfully through these massive sandhills. It does not matter if Old Tom or English Tom gets most of the credit for the design, the holes are great. The 6th green, with the snaking burn in front, is a work of art.

The physical and spiritual heart of Cruden Bay is the 8th. Tom Simpson called it "an outstanding jewel of a hole, mischievous, subtle and provocative, the element of luck with the tee shot being very high." The 8th green does indeed sit like a jewel at the base of the towering gorse covered hills. Par in Scotland is irrelevant in many ways, but I love the fact that the short 8th, only 250 yards, remains a par four. To its credit, the club has nev-

er changed anything about the hole. In a lifetime of playing this game, it remains one of my favorite holes. The fact that I made an eagle 2 on it in 1994 has absolutely no influence on my feelings.

The view from the 8th green across the 16th hole, to the beach and ocean beyond, is breathtaking. As you make the steep ascent to the new 9th tee, it becomes apparent that the prior scene was a mere prelude of the glorious vista to come. The climb to the 9th tee at Cruden Bay is arduous, one of the toughest I have experienced. However, the reward that awaits more than compensates for the struggle.

A few years ago, in a brilliant move, the 9th hole was shifted about 100 yards to the east, right along the edge of the highest point on the course. As a result, an average par four was transformed into a great and memorable hole. For me, along with the 4th tee at Shiskine and the 11th tee at Dunaverty, the 9th tee at Cruden Bay is one of the spiritual hearts of golf. You can't help but sit down and take it all in for a few minutes, most likely in stunned silence—and not simply because you are exhausted from the ascent.

When the new 9th hole was created, the 10th tee was moved about 50 yards to the west. As an added benefit, this has made the 10th a much better hole. Driving from the 10th tee to the valley floor below is a singular thrill. It is a wonderful and testing par four, usually played in a strong crosswind.

The 11th and 12th are often said to be the weak link in a stretch of otherwise wonderful golf holes. As we putted on the 12th, I noticed what appeared to be another green in the distance amidst the bright yellow gorse, set against the sparkling blue ocean. This hidden green was yet another addition since my last visit. I made a mental note to try to find out more about it.

The 13th runs along the ocean and is a great par five. The tee shot must avoid a winding burn and high grass along the beach. The second shot should be played to the left side of the fairway to open the best approach into the massive green, which lies at the base of the dune from which we have just descended. The 14th is another singular hole in my golfing experience. The tee shot is played blind, from an elevated tee hard by the beach, to a fairway that appears to be non-existent. The near vertical gorse-covered dune is there to destroy any tee shot that, as my great Prestwick caddie Chris McBride once said, "has Left-wing tendencies."

From the fairway, should it be found, one of the great blind shots in golf awaits. The almost rectangular shaped green is located over a dune down in a sunken pit, at least 15 feet below the surrounding ground. I have never seen another green like this one. If you don't have a smile on your face after playing this hole, then you probably should not be playing golf at Cruden Bay.

I have always viewed the 15th and 16th holes as two sides of the same coin. Back-to-back short holes, they continue the glorious madness that Old Tom and Tom Simpson have so thoroughly maintained throughout the round. The 195-yard 15th is played over the steep corner of the ever-present mountainous dune, blind and dog-legged, to a delightfully hidden green. Over the years, I have hit everything from a full driver to a 9-iron on this hole. It is psychedelic madness that breaks every rule of modern golf design. It is also pure fun. The 16th finally breaks us free of the great dune's clutches and is somewhat more conventional. It is played from an elevated tee to a picturesque green set amongst the rolling dunes. I once scored 13 on this hole in a 40-mph crosswind, en route to a score of 106, with tee shot after tee shot flying wildly onto the beach. The very next morning, in dead calm conditions, I made a tap-in birdie 2, on the way to shooting a 75. That ridiculous 31 shot reversal succinctly describes the joyous vagaries of links golf.

The 17th and 18th are good holes, though not as good as their predecessors, and serve mainly to take us out of the mighty duneland back to the clubhouse. The tee shot on the 17th must avoid an unusual grass covered mound in the middle of the fairway, thought to be the burial ground of Scots and Danes killed in the Battle of Cruden Bay in 1012. The tee shot on the 18th should favor the left for the best angle into the green, but out of bounds lurks along that entire side. We shook hands with our new friend Chris and invited him to join us for lunch, upstairs in the clubhouse bar.

We climbed the stairs to the 2nd floor and the lovely glass walled dining area to be greeted by a large multi-colored sign, which read:

*Happy Birthday Jake.*

Not enough can be said about the hospitality shown to us by the staff that day at Cruden Bay. It is something both of us will never forget. We had a delicious lunch, complete with a requisite pint of Tennent's. As we were finishing up our meal, the strains of the Happy Birthday song started to play over the sound system—the bar staff had inserted Jake's name into the song. The staff came out to our table with a shortbread and strawberry cake complete with a large birthday candle.

Les Durno, then the club's general manager, also appeared along with the cake and introduced himself. A man who obviously loves Cruden Bay, we immediately struck up a conversation about the history of the course, the old railway hotel, and the brilliant changes to the 9th and 10th. I mentioned that I thought the new 9th hole had put Cruden Bay at an even higher level in the golf world.

"Aye, it has indeed," he replied. "I remember walking out into the gorse with the architect on his first visit. You could see what a great hole it would be before we even started work. It's been a brilliant change to the course."

Curious about the hidden green I had seen behind the 12th, I asked Les about it. A smile lit up his face, "Ah, yes. That's the alternate 12th hole. We play it in the winter. There are some that would love to make it a permanent hole, with some possible reworking of the 11th and 12th. You should play it when you go back out this afternoon. The tee is up in the dunes to the right." Of course, we went back around after lunch and played the hole. It is tremendous and it would not surprise me if it became a permanent part of the routing at some point.

Les and I continued our splendid conversation for several more minutes, with the old Victorian clubhouse and demolished railway hotel the main topics. He then took me to meet the wonderful booking secretary Elaine Stephens, who I remembered talking to on the phone all those years ago in 1994. We spoke briefly about the old days of £30 day tickets, fax machines, and real, written letters for booking golf reservations. As I was leaving to join Jake for another birthday trip around this wonderful links, Elaine said, "I am so pleased you made it back to Cruden Bay."

Twenty years was far too long to miss the wonders of Cruden Bay. Despite the passage of time and the inevitable changes it brings, it has stayed true to its roots. It is my dad's favorite golf course. That is good enough for me.

# 9

# Cullen

## Golf on Mars

"... This is not typical links land, because on several holes the golfer has to negotiate abandoned sea-cliffs and stacks. These upstanding rock ridges cause the player to make blind shots on the 12th, 13th and 14th holes and if the golf ball hits any of the almost vertical rock faces, it can fly in almost any direction."
—Robert Price, *Scotland's Golf Courses*

There comes a moment early in a round of golf at Cullen Links where a first-time visitor realizes they are about to experience something unique. The 1st hole, in the best Scottish tradition, is a pleasant, flat and unassuming 345-yard par four that serves to ease players into the round and away from the clubhouse. An abandoned railway line borders the left side, but there is plenty of room to the right. It's a welcoming, easy hole. Climbing to the 2nd tee, the uninitiated golfer may become confused as to how to proceed. When Tron Carter of the American multi-media golf group No Laying Up played Cullen for the first time with longtime member, club champion, fundraiser and ambassador George Clark, he asked, "Where is the green?"

Clark silently pointed north, seemingly straight into the sky. Carter responded to the gesture with a laugh, "There is no way."

Clark, with a reserved smile, replied:

"Yeah, up there."

Located 60 miles northwest of Aberdeen via the A96, B9022 and A98, the Cullen Links Golf Club was founded in 1870. The entry drive, under a massive solid masonry railway viaduct constructed in 1884, signals that a special day is at hand. Originally laid out by the brilliant Old Tom Morris, the course moves wildly through linksland, moorland, post-glacial cliffs and eroded prehistoric red rock formations. All this excitement occurs hard by Cullen Bay on the North Sea, which is in full and glorious view from every hole on the course. In geology professor Robert Price's seminal 1989 book, *"Scotland's Golf Courses"*, the varied landforms of Cullen are categorized as: raised platform, cliff, stack and raised beach—and disused railway. The brilliant routing takes full advantage of each one of these assorted geological conditions. You will play shots at Cullen that would be hard to imagine in even your wildest golf dreams.

Cullen has often been overlooked in some of the more well-known Scottish golf books. It does not even rate a mention by American James Finegan in his classic *"Blasted Heaths and Blessed Greens,"* and only receives a passing reference in the wonderful *"The Scottish Golf Guide"* by Glasgow native David Hamilton. These are both writers that took pride in highlighting the smaller, lesser-known courses of Scotland. With renewed interest recently in the experience of playing fun, affordable and traditional Scottish courses, places like Cullen are being increasingly recognized for the rare treasures that they are.

Tron Carter (aka Todd Schuster) enjoys logistics and the pleasurable anticipation of golf trip planning. As No Laying Up's unofficial travel coordinator, he handled the preparations for a 2018 Scotland trip to film the group's popular YouTube travel series, *Tourist Sauce*. It was important to Carter that the experience included all levels of Scottish golf. Consulting Tom Doak's Confidential Guide to Golf Courses for inspiration, he found a review of the links, which he recalls mentioning Cullen only briefly as "crazy" with "wild and intriguing criss-crossing holes." That description interested him enough to look up the course on Google Earth. "After I saw the place on Google, I just went down a wormhole and got on the club website. I was very intrigued. Visit Scotland helped us out with planning our trip. They thought I'd made a mistake when I asked that we visit Cullen," recalls Carter.

With an ambitious itinerary that included Cruden Bay Golf Club and Cullen on the same day, the travelers were understandably feeling a little weary as they pulled into the beautiful seaside town of Cullen on a gray, overcast afternoon. The group's mood was immediately lifted as the sun came out almost on cue as they approached the old railway viaduct—which dramatically signals the entrance to Cullen Links. Phil Landes, aka "Big Randy" of No Laying Up, vividly remembers the drive into the club:

> "I had absolutely no expectations or any idea what Cullen would be like. The entire east coast of Scotland was just so idyllic and interesting to me. I think that feeling only grew stronger the closer I got to Cullen. When I saw that old aqueduct—I really don't know what possessed me—I climbed up there to look around. We had a little time to kill, so the first thing I wanted to do is climb up there and just look around and it was just so cool. You see the little unassuming parking lot, you see the clubhouse, you see the course, the town and the ocean—it's just all so perfectly Scottish in all the best ways."

Tron, Big Randy, and the other two members of the group, Chris "Soly" Solomon and Dennis "DJ" Piehowski, were met in the clubhouse (where green fees are paid at the bar) by George Clark and his wife Anne. Drafted as the NLU playing partner and guide for the day, George was born in Cullen and started learning the game on the course around age seven, as most Cullen youngsters did in those days. He is a two-time club champion, while

Anne has won the Ladies title a remarkable 19 times. George now lives in Aberdeen, where he is a member of the excellent Murcar Links. His emotional connection to his home club is so strong that in years past he would often make the hour and 20-minute drive north to Cullen to play his golf, bypassing much closer options.

George is a quiet, thoughtful man who can quote Bob Dylan concert setlists at will. He was initially skeptical of the group of young American golfers. Cullen was not on the standard itinerary of most visitors to Scotland, especially a popular American media group filming a series about Scottish links golf. "The first few holes, I know George thought we were trying to make fun of the place. I don't think he understood why we had come to Cullen. He thought it was all some kind of practical joke," says Tron. The Scots have a respectful attitude towards all types of golf courses. As much credence is given to a 4,623-yard, par 63 layout like Cullen as it is to an internationally renowned links such as Muirfield. Clark soon realized he was mistaken in his initial assessment of his playing partners, "It became apparent that the guys of NLU had the 'Scotland feel' for golf and the modest privilege of playing a course such as Cullen. Any reservations I may have had soon disappeared as the golf course spoke for itself—and they were eager listeners."

Having played an enjoyable and quick—we never seemed rushed—round at Cullen with George and Jake in 2019, I can attest to the club's seductive charms. Unlike No Laying Up, we had high expectations for Cullen. These were exceeded at every turn. George greeted us like old friends on that brilliant May afternoon, which seems like another lifetime now, in the inviting and convivial clubhouse. Hearing that we still needed our lunch, he immediately went into the kitchen to speak to the staff to sort us some soup and a ham & cheese toastie. Without being asked, he brought Jake a pint of Tennent's. In a world that has become increasingly bereft of manners and gentlemen, George Clark is a role model. He has promoted Cullen tirelessly, humbly and modestly, letting the club and course speak for itself.

Like a Shakespearean play, Cullen Links is a drama in five

acts. The 1st hole is clearly the first act, often known as the exposition. Like many great opening acts, it is a subtle precursor and introduction of the story to come. An opening birdie is a possibility. The 2nd hole, a 121 yard par three that baffled Mr. Schuster, quickly starts the second act in which the action escalates. We play straight up into the sky, over rough ground, to a small green surrounded by trouble. It is an intimidating tee shot and a great hole.

Climbing to the heights of the 2nd green, we have now reached the upper moorland level of Cullen. This is the heart of the venerable links' brilliant second act, which continues through hole 10. Holes 3 through 6 are played along on this high plateau, offering some of the most spectacular views to be found in Scotland. The town of Cullen lies in the distance, along the curve of the bay, and even hasty Scots will forgive you for stopping briefly to take in the majestic scene. The 6th, aptly called "Bay View" is a lovely 181-yard par three that plays to a green situated along the cliff's edge and adjacent to the 7th tee.

The 7th tee at Cullen is wonderful. Called "Firth View," it manages to surpass the visual splendor of its predecessor. The tee shot drops thrillingly over 90 feet from tee to green. A steep walking path takes us back down to the lower beach level. It is a strict

par three of 224 yards, but a bogey 4 will often be good enough to defeat your opponent. Carter perfectly sums up the 7th and the essence of "par" at Cullen Links, "I'm not sure what the par is at Cullen. It doesn't really matter, does it? It's not formulaic. It's not templated. It's very wild and different. It's only 4,500 yards or so. That doesn't mean it's easy, right? You still have to play the shots and get the ball in the hole."

Firmly back in the lowlands now, at beach level, we continue to progress through the second act of Cullen, as it builds slowly and steadily towards the apex. The 9th hole, like the scenes of many great plays, brilliantly foreshadows the upcoming climax of the third act. An elevated tee is the foundation for this 195-yard par three that plays straight out to the ocean, at the mercy of the wind. Walking down this fairway discussing the understated brilliance of Bob Dylan's last album with George Clark, with the seemingly endless Cullen Bay serving as backdrop, is one of the highlights of my golfing life. The 9th is my favorite hole at Cullen.

The 10th hole is a lovely 311-yard par four that plays along and slightly above the strand. It is a worthy transition to the third act and climax of Cullen—the 11th through the 13th holes. This triumvirate of par threes—245, 179, and 152 yards respectively—is unparalleled in Scottish golf. Each hole plays into, over and around tall, vertical red rock monoliths which are remnants of ancient glacial erosion, the sea stacks of Robert Price's book. The only other course I have seen with this type of geological feature lies just up the coast at the relatively new Covesea Links. It is reminiscent of a scene out of a science fiction movie set on Mars, strangely haunting and beautiful.

The 11th green is set in a natural punchbowl directly in front of one of the large red standing stones. For the first-time visitor, the backdrop to the green is almost a shock to the senses. It is a surreal setting and a preview of the holes to come. The tee shot on the 12th plays over the corner of the 11th green and must negotiate multiple rock structures. It is gloriously blind, as is its successor. The 13th, aptly named Red Craig, ends Cullen's climatic third act with another tee shot directly over the tallest of all the red monoliths to a small, perfectly placed green. A par on any of the holes in this enigmatic triumvirate is an accomplishment to be remembered.

This level of excitement must start to diminish, but only gradually, as we enter the fourth act of Cullen—the 14th thru 16th. The 14th is a 206-yard par three that plays past the towering red craig and back out to Cullen Bay. The 15th is the only par five on the course and starts with a beachside tee. It stretches along the bay for 511 yards. Another beachside tee initiates the 16th, the shot played back across the 15th fairway in true Cullen fashion. The green is protected by three small pot bunkers and is a lovely spot to pause and take in the outlandish craggy landscape one final time before turning south for home.

The fifth and final act—the resolution—is the 17th and 18th holes. Like the 1st hole, they serve an intended purpose. "You know, 17 and 18 are just kind of flattish par fours, but by that point you are so taken by the place, and you probably have a great match going, that you are just hitting golf shots and having fun. There is no box that you can put Cullen in," says Schuster. The 17th, a 270-yard par four, is a definite birdie opportunity. The 18th parallels the 1st like a mirror image of the first and last at

the Old Course. With the old railway viaduct providing the back-drop for the final scene at Cullen Links, it is the ideal finishing hole for this course.

On a trip that included some of the high holy places of Scottish golf, Cullen became an unexpected highlight for the No Laying Up crew. "When people travel to Scotland and just want to check all the famous places off the list, that's fine, but I think that can wear you down some. And you are missing out on a lot of what is so great about Scotland," says Schuster. Phil Landes eloquently describes his feelings about Cullen, "Playing with George increased our experience ten-fold. Cullen is so much more than just golf. When you meet a person like George and you see what the golf course means to the community of Cullen, it's almost like we got to be Scottish for five hours. You feel like you are part of the fabric of daily life. Travel is about exploring and finding new things and meeting new people. Golf needs places like Cullen."

As for George Clark, the experience of introducing his beloved course to a group of rabid young American golfers also affected him. "Afterwards, I felt that in order to preserve the past, there is a need to embrace the present," he says. Cullen is surviving, and thriving, now. Clark gives a lot of credit to the No Laying Up crew. "The effect of NLU is ongoing. In immediate terms, visitor

numbers were up by about 15 percent the next year after the film. It has made Cullen more well-known and more of a player in Northeast Scotland golf," he says. Carter, for his part, deflects any praise for his group. With admiration in his voice, he sums up his feelings about Cullen:

> "Scotland has such a deep bench of great golf courses—more than any other country. Cullen may not be on anybody's top 10 list, but sometimes those are the best places to visit. The welcome and hospitality are 100 percent genuine. Cullen just is a magical, unique and authentic place."

Nature is the ultimate golf course designer. Old Tom Morris had the eyes to see it. We are fortunate it has not changed since the Great Man walked these shores over 125 years ago.

Jake and I went back to Cullen in 2023, in no small part to stay at The Royal Oak Hotel, which makes a claim as the originator of that uniquely Scottish delicacy, Cullen Skink. This thick soup, made with smoked haddock, potatoes and leeks has been a long-time favorite of ours. We were not disappointed. I have made it at home over the years, trying to adapt it to what is readily available in the U.S.A. This is my version. It takes a little extra time, but smoking the haddock is critical to the recipe.

CULLEN SKINK

3 large smoked haddock fillets (Cold smoked ahead
of time on indirect heat at 200 F for 2 hours on a Big
Green Egg or other smoker)
8 cups whole milk
2 bay leaves
2 tbs butter
3 large leeks, sliced (white part only)
6 Yukon Gold potatoes, cubed
1 cup cream
Sea salt and black pepper

Saute the leeks in butter until tender in a large stock
pot. Add the milk, bay leaves and whole smoked haddock
fillets to the pot. Simmer for about 10-15 minutes then
scoop out the fish. Add the diced potatoes, salt and pepper, and cover. Simmer until the potatoes are very tender.
Blend the soup with a few pulses of an immersion blender,
leaving leeks and potatoes chunky. Flake the fish and add
back to the soup. Add the cream and heat until it is almost
boiling. Add a bit more salt and pepper, if needed. Serve
with brown bread.

## Echoes in the Wind:

## Mathew Goggin and the Final Round of the 2009 Open Championship

> "Sorrow is soon enough when it comes."
> —Ancient Scottish Proverb

On a cold, rainy morning in April 2023, on the way down the A77 to Portpatrick, I passed a small sign for the road to Turnberry. As it has forever done, the dark mass of the Ailisa Craig loomed on the horizon, bearing mute witness to history. It was 6 a.m. when I arrived. The car park by the putting green and 1st tee was empty. I walked out into the misting rain to the 18th green. Without the massive Open grandstands, it all looked smaller somehow. My last visit to Turnberry had been in August 2000, when I played a memorable round with my dad and cousin Chris. Much had changed in the intervening years, but the remarkable history of The Open at the Ailsa course remains.

Turnberry has played a seminal role in my now 47-year obsession with Scottish links golf. The famous Duel in the Sun, as the 1977 Open Championship is known, is considered by many to be the greatest tournament in golf history. I watched the final two rounds with my dad—the Open was his favorite tournament.

Nicklaus and Watson were like titans to a 10-year-old growing up in Alabama. They just jumped off the television screen. The course was burnt out to a crispy brownish green. The ball rolled forever. I decided that this was the way golf was meant to be played.

Watson won with a tenacious combination of miraculous putting and beautiful iron shots. I was a Nicklaus fanatic, but Watson won my respect that day. That last round was simply the greatest spectacle I had ever witnessed. The greatest golfer of all time shot 65-66 over the last two days, and it wasn't enough. Watson shot 65-65 to beat him by a stroke. Alabama native Hubert Green finished in 3rd place—a full 10 strokes behind Nicklaus.

Thirty-two years later, I watched the final round of the 2009 Open at Turnberry with my three boys. Incredibly, impossibly, unimaginably, Tom Watson, at age 59, had a chance to win his 6th Open title and tie the great Harry Vardon. We gathered around the television in my small book filled office to watch the last few holes. We cheered when Tom birdied the 71st hole to take the lead, and then again when he hit a perfect drive on the 72nd. We yelled, almost in unison, when Watson's fateful 8-iron approach landed about a foot from perfection. The end was heartbreaking to watch.

Finding the spot where Watson had played his third shot almost 15 years before, I stood in a silent reverie for a few minutes. A massive Scottish flag flapped wildly in the breeze. The severity of the slope up to the green surprised me. It had looked much flatter on television. I had always wondered if Watson had played the correct shot—from this exact spot where I now stood. I had often thought about what went wrong on his perfectly stuck 2nd shot. Through the chance meeting of a close friend and professional golfer Mathew Goggin at Landmand Golf Club in Nebraska, I suddenly had an opportunity to get a unique perspective on what happened that day.

In July 2009, on a windy Sunday afternoon, a 59-year-old man came within one hard linksland bounce of perhaps the greatest achievement in the history of sport. Mathew Goggin, a 35-year-old professional golfer, was his playing partner.

Mat Goggin comes from a golf loving family on the small Australian island of Tasmania. His mother, an excellent golfer, and his grandfather helped introduce him to the game as a young child. However, he didn't become obsessed with the game at that early age. He preferred other sports like tennis. It was at a tennis tournament with his mates, around the age of 13, that he became hooked on golf.

"Some of my friends wanted to play golf one day after the tennis. You know how it happens. I had a few decent whacks that day and, all of a sudden, I was obsessed with it," he recalls.

Before too long his game started to improve dramatically and he joined the Australian Institute of Sport. The organization had a fledgling, full-time, golf program where kids lived in Melbourne and played all the great sand belt courses. The curriculum included sports science and psychology components, which were very experimental for the time. He gives a lot of credit to his time at the institute. "I was sort of this talented, raw player. By the end of that program, within twelve months of leaving it, I was one of the best amateurs in the world. I don't think it would've ever happened for me without it, because there was just no pathway coming out of Tasmania," says Goggin.

In the summer of 1995, Goggin won both the Tasmanian and Australian Amateur. He was medalist in the Canadian Amateur, which allowed him to play in several Australian professional events. While working for his father cleaning out horse stables, he realized he would have made more money that summer as a professional golfer. "I think I would've earned around $12,000 based on my results and I sort of said to my Dad, you know I think it's time I turned pro instead of making 10 bucks an hour mucking out stables." In a few weeks, he had qualified for the Asian Tour, before moving onto the European Challenge Tour—winning an event in both 1996 and 1997. Goggin acquired his European Tour card and played there for two years, with some success. In 1998, he came to the United States to play what was then called the Nike Tour, where he won twice in 1999. His position on the Nike Tour money list that season provided him with his PGA Tour card, and he was a member of the world's biggest tour until 2010. He qualified for the 2009 Open at Turnberry based on his world ranking points.

It was a sunny, breezy afternoon when Mat Goggin stepped onto the 1st tee of the Ailsa course with the legendary Tom Watson—in the final game of the Open Championship. The Tasmanian was in 2nd place, a single stroke behind his playing partner. A brilliant 69 in the third round had moved him to 3-under for the tournament.

"I absolutely flushed it on Saturday. I really hit a lot of good shots. I remember I played with Martin Kaymer and his caddie was an Australian guy who had caddied for me before. It was just a pretty relaxed day and I played really well. It wasn't some crazy round where you make a bunch of putts. It was just very windy, tough conditions and I hit a lot of great shots and sort of stacked a really good round together," he remembers. Ivor Robson, the iconic starter for the Royal & Ancient, greeted Watson like an old friend. Goggin was focused on the task at hand. The pairing with the American legend had not affected him. "To be honest, I wasn't giving it any thought. He was just another player," he recalls, "I wasn't intimidated. The moment is intimidating enough without worrying who you are playing with. That opening tee shot is as big as it can possibly get. That is way harder than a shot on 15 or 16 when you actually have a chance to win. You are in the flow then."

As you would expect on the exposed linksland of the Ayrshire coast, the wind had been a major factor for the entire week on the hard, dry links. Goggin feels that strong crosswinds are what made it so difficult. "There aren't many holes that go directly into the wind. It was always very hard across or hard across and down. Every shot had to work with or against the wind," Goggin says. "If you had the wrong spin, the ball was just gone."

The Scottish crowd on the 1st tee was in a state of near hysteria over the thought of Watson winning the Open. Shouts of "Come on, Tooooom!" started early and only increased in volume throughout the round. The two competitors spoke convivially as they walked down the fairway, but each soon moved into his own world. This was the final round of the world's greatest championship.

Both men got off to a nervous start. A couple of loose shots had them both at 2-over for the round after four holes—they were now trailing Ross Fisher of England. This was not going to be a day when a single man seized control—the conditions were just too difficult. After two good tee shots into the tough 231-yard 6th, Tappie Toorie, the pair seemed to settle into the round. Birdies for both on the par-five 7th and the final group was squarely back in contention for the Claret Jug.

Almost 15 years later, Goggin is still amazed at the way the 59-year-old Watson struck his driver, playing it on almost every hole when others resorted to hybrids and long irons.

"A lot of the times when you've got that cross breeze, the difference between slightly riding it or slightly holding up against it can be 50, 60, 70 yards. Tom had very little spin on his drives. Almost no spin. You know, in some cases if you try to hold it against the breeze, you are basically not going to be able to reach some of the par fours in two. I was hitting it sort of 50 yards right and hoping that it would come back on the fairway. And then Tom would hit his driver and would start at like right center, and it would stay right there and not move. It was like—well perfect, it was a perfect ball flight. He was just a machine with his driver. And he got it out there, too."

Goggin shot a solid 36 on the opening nine to Watson's 37—both men were now at 2-under and trailing European Ryder Cup stalwart Lee Westwood by a single shot. The wind was only increasing as the afternoon continued. After a wonderful approach to the 452-yard 10th, Goggin made birdie. He was now tied for the lead in the Open Championship. Much to the delight of the pro-Watson crowd, Tom followed up with a great birdie on the par three 11th. There was now a three-way tie at the top of the leaderboard:

> Lee Westwood -3
> Tom Watson -3
> Mathew Goggin -3

The Tasmanian recalls being mostly unaware of his position at that point in the round.

> "I really didn't know. I was never a big scoreboard watcher. I don't even remember looking at a leaderboard coming in. I knew how I stood in relation to Tom and I suspected we were right there because of the crowd's reaction—and I knew that nobody was going to shoot a crazy low score in that wind."

With both men now playing solid, confident golf, the pace of play suddenly slowed. This was not an ideal development for two of the fastest golfers in the field. Goggin took it in stride. The delay did offer the twosome a few more chances to have another amiable chat or two. "We talked about the Kansas City Royals quite a lot for some reason," he says with a laugh. Still tied for the lead, Goggin hit a lovely wedge to 10 feet on the 13th. Watson hit a tremendous lag putt from 40 feet for a tap-in par. The cheers were now reaching levels not heard on the Ayrshire coast since The Duel in the Sun itself—an event that had taken place an unthinkable 32 years earlier.

The 34-year-old from Tasmania now had a straight uphill putt to take the solo lead in the championship. He pushed it slightly right and the wind took it away. "I just hit a terrible putt. It wasn't hit with any authority," he recalls.

On the 14th tee, Goggin hit his best drive of the day, beautifully turning a boring draw into the howling left to right wind. He was left with 195 yards to the hole. The normally expedient player took the most time of the day over the shot, discussing it at length with his caddie. It was one of the most critical moments of his championship.

> "We took so much time on that shot because it was the exact same shot that I had the day before. I had hit a bullet 4-iron a day earlier and it nearly flew the green, but it finished up just perfectly. The wind was slightly different, and we were discussing whether to hit 3-iron. I thought if I caught it just right, it would be gone. We wound up going with a 4-iron again. I thought I flushed it. It felt great, but at the end the wind took it, and it was gone."

The ball wound up in a bunker and Goggin did well to blast it out to eight feet. The wind seemed to bother him again over his putt and he missed, making bogey. Watson also bogeyed. They now trailed Westwood by a shot, who was just ahead in the penultimate game.

Ca' Canny, the 206-yard 15th, proved to be the downfall of Matt Goggin's brilliant run at Turnberry. It was the scene of Watson's miraculous 60-foot putt from off the green in 1977, just when the great Nicklaus had appeared poised to put him away for good. The two players stood and watched as Westwood made a bogey from the back bunker, a spot that had troubled players the entire day. With the hole playing straight downwind, Watson, the consummate links player, played a safe shot to 30 feet short of the extreme back hole location. Goggin followed with a dead flushed 7-iron that landed 25 feet short of the flag and almost hit the hole. He watched from the tee as his ball trickled inexorably into the back bunker, like droplets of water from a leaking faucet. It was the turning point of the championship for him.

"I had a good yardage. I had a perfect 7-iron yardage. I'm just like, I can just hit this as hard as I want. It's just going to land on top. And I just smoked it straight at the flag. I mean, I thought it was perfect. It only just trickled into the bunker, too. It was just like—it went in so slowly. The funny thing about that is we were standing on that tee for a while, and I remember watching. I hit it exactly where Lee had just been and it's not actually a hard bunker shot. I was looking at it like, this is not a hard shot. Then I shuffled my feet over the shot and the sand is that very heavy beach sand. I go to hit the bunker shot, there's no sand underneath the ball. Aah, I can see why the exact same thing happened to Lee. I've never asked him about it, but I'm sure it's the same thing. You're thinking, well, I've got to give this a bit of a thump with this heavy sand. And then you do and there's no sand underneath—it's baked out like. The club just bounced."

Goggin's sand shot led to another bogey. Watson, who was now like a specter of Harry Vardon come to life and walking the links of Ayrshire once again, lagged his birdie putt close for an easy par. He now led Goggin by a stroke. Up ahead on the 17th green, Florence, Alabama native Stewart Cink missed a birdie putt to stay at 1-under. The then 5-time PGA Tour winner had not really been any part of the television broadcast drama, but he was only a shot off the lead.

The 16th hole, a 445-yarder called Wee Burn, is one of the most recognizable holes in golf. Up ahead of the final group, Westwood made a bogey to drop back to 1-under. Almost inconceivably, Tom Watson now had the solo lead in the Open Championship with only three holes to play. Goggin seemed deflated after his bogey on the 15th. He hit his worst shot of the day, missing the green badly to the left. Mat Goggin's chances of winning The Open slipped away as he made another bogey to fall to even par. Watson was looking confident now. He hit a textbook approach shot to 30 feet past the hole, to avoid the burn. After he made a testing par putt to retain the lead at 2-under, Peter Alliss of the BBC exclaimed,

"My God, can this really happen?"

On the 18th green, Cink played a long iron approach which managed to stop almost exactly where it landed. The shot was a great one, but curiously the hole had suddenly played straight into the wind. That would not be the case in roughly 30 minutes. Cink made the short birdie putt to finish the tournament at 2-under and in a tie for the lead. Back on the par-five 17th fairway, Watson hit a brilliant hybrid shot that trickled just over the back of the green, no more than 40 feet from the hole. "That second shot Tom hit on 17 was just a bullet," says Goggin. Watson played his third with a putter from off the green, hitting it close and tapping in for birdie. He now held the lead at 3-under, with only one hole to play.

As he stood by the 18th tee, Goggin realized he wasn't going to win. This was the first time all day that he considered what might be happening with his legendary playing partner.

> "I hadn't really thought about it much all day because he's just another golfer, you know what I mean? He's your competitor, you're out there, you're playing, it's just another round of golf—even though it's not. On the 18th tee, I kind of turned around to Brian, my caddie, and said I can't believe this is going to happen. This is kind of crazy. But yeah, I had kind of stuffed it up for myself a few holes earlier, then he stuffed it up for himself—and then for me again as well—because then everyone was saying, you could've been there when he won! But I was like, well, I wanted to be there for when I won—but that would have been alright to see."

Almost everyone reading this story will recall what happened on the 72nd hole. For many golf fans, it is burned into their memory—something that some of the most ardent Tom Watson fans are still reluctant to talk about to this day. Goggin was amazed by Watson's drive on the 18th. "I couldn't believe he was hitting his Adams rescue club. I was thinking, why would you even bring that bunker into play? Literally, I hit a five iron and a seven iron on that hole. If you hit a five iron, like, the fairway is 100 yards wide. And then he just absolutely rips it up there past the bunker, a perfect shot."

Watson's approach shot on 18, a hole renamed Duel in the Sun in 2004—has been analyzed by golf fans for almost 15 years now. Goggin recalls that there had been a few terse discussions between Watson and his caddie throughout the round, but he does not attribute any of that to the club selection on 18. Goggin recalls his thoughts as he watched Watson's ill-fated approach:

> "The only way to play that shot—you just had to land it short of the green, to be honest. That green is a bit of a triangle shape. The pin was just back middle—or maybe just a little back middle right. But you couldn't land it very far on the green. If you wanted to hit it into the middle of the green, you had to carry it a good 10 feet on. I hit 7-iron from 200 and something meters—it was crazy. It just trickled on the front of the green. I think Tom just hit too good of a shot and it landed in the wrong spot on the front of the green. But I mean, the question for me is, should he even be trying to hit it back there?" It's one of those flags where it was so firm, so fast, so windy, that a sort of benign flag actually became tricky."

The greatest links player of the modern era hit a perfectly stuck 8-iron that bounded over the green and trickled inexorably, tragically, over the back. Tom Watson had two shots to win a record tying 6th Open Championship at the unthinkable age of 59—an age when most players are not even competitive on the Senior tours. Mat Goggin applauded his competitor as he reached the green. The cheers could probably be heard 20 miles away on the ancient links of Prestwick. Watson chose a putter for his third shot, another subject of debate between links golf fans. Goggin has a theory for why Watson did not chip from this spot—the riskier shot he believes would have been the best option to hit close to the hole:

> "In fairness, he had not chipped the ball well. I would say at age 59, he was not chipping like Tom Watson in his 20s and 30s, right? Every chip he hit was to 10 feet. He just made almost all the putts. He didn't chip the ball stone dead at all. I think that putting it through a sort of sketchy lie and the fringe grass on 17—where he knocks it stone dead—all of a sudden, that made him think, I should really putt this one. In reality, it was straight back into the breeze. They'd had quite a bit of rain, so the first cut was immaculate in its parts, and over the back of 18 was one of those parts where it's perfect—so you've got perfect grass. The only difficulty in the chip is that it has a slight mound and then it rolls down. But then it's very flat around the hole. Again, you're chipping back into the breeze, it's almost back uphill with a perfect lie into a strong breeze. So if you don't catch it thin, it's a very straightforward chip. But I think, because he had so much success with the putter, especially on 17, he decided to go with that. As soon as he hit that shot, the energy just drained out of him."

Watson's putt ran eight feet past the hole. Goggin lipped out from 60 feet to finish the tournament at even par 280, in a tie for 5th place with Luke Donald and Retief Goosen, a finish which got him into the 2010 Masters. He picked up his ball from the hole as Watson lined up a putt to win The Open Championship. "The momentum was gone. I could feel it. I wanted him to make the putt, but I admit that I didn't have a good feeling about it," he remembers. To the horror of the Scottish crowd, Watson badly missed the winning putt. It was his worst putting stroke of the day. He limped through the 4-hole aggregate playoff, eventually losing by six shots to Stewart Cink, who became The Champion Golfer of the Year. Harry Vardon's record was safe, perhaps for eternity.

Goggin has practiced hard the last few years to make a comeback on the Champions Tour, playing a few events in Australia to prepare for his 50th birthday that came in July 2024. He has overcome some injuries in his mid-40s that kept him from being able to practice for several years. "I feel as good as I have in a long time," he says. His love of the great Sandbelt courses of Australia—and his experiences in the Open Championship—have led to an interest in golf course architecture and the development of courses in his native Tasmania. He is a bit philosophical about what happened back in 2009. "Some people say that Tom deserved to win, that his second shot on 18 was perfect. It reminds me of the line from that Clint Eastwood movie *Unforgiven*—deserve has got nothing to do with it. That's just links golf. I am sure Tom would tell you the same thing."

There are ghosts at Turnberry. I closed my eyes, and I could hear the echoes of the delirious roars of the Scottish crowd when the mighty Nicklaus made that impossible, ridiculous, birdie on the 72nd hole in 1977. I could see the two Americans walking off the 18th green, arm in arm, while the crowd continued to stand and cheer in wondrous admiration. It all happened right where I was standing.

The opposite side of that joyous scene was 2009, when a miracle slipped through the fingers of one of golf's greatest legends. Mat Goggin saw it all unfold firsthand, and this is how he remembers it nearly 15 years later. In his mind, it was not bad luck that cost the golf world a fairy tale ending. It was links golf, and it was just not meant to be. Golf and life often work that way. Maybe the arcane forces that seem to govern links golf in Scotland decreed that it was simply just too much for a 59-year-old man to win the world's greatest championship for a sixth time. Even in a crushing loss, Tom Watson gave all of us hope to keep searching for that perfect round of golf.

I turned away from the green. The stately old white hotel sat high on the hill, shrouded in mist. The greenskeepers were coming out to prepare for the day. I walked back to my car and continued the drive to Portpatrick.

Southend, Kintyre, from Dunaverty.

21582

# 10

## Dunaverty

# The Links My Soul Loves Best

*"In memory of Jordan Hartsell*
*The best golfer I ever saw*
*by Jim Hartsell, his Dad"*
—Bench on the 11th tee at Dunaverty Golf Club

Overlooking Dunaverty Bay, the abandoned Keil Hotel sits near the base of Cnoc Mor like the ghost of an ancient ocean liner. The art deco lines of the stark white building remain elegant and restrained despite the cruel passage of time. The sky turns orange, then bright red, as the sun slowly descends over the Mull of Kintyre. The world for which this proud structure was built no longer exists. In Southend, Scotland, that world is not forgotten.

Based on a design by Glasgow architect James Austin-Laird, construction of the hotel began in 1938. While the hotel was under construction it was taken over by the British Navy at the outset of World War II for use as a hospital. The bright white stucco exterior was a welcome beacon for planes and ships at a time when lighthouses around the country were extinguished as a wartime safety precaution. The navy fitted out the interior to accommodate wounded sailors and used the building until the end of the war.

Local resident Captain James Taylor finally opened it as a working hotel in 1947. It operated successfully until the late 1960s when UK holiday goers largely abandoned these types of places for the sunnier climates of Portugal and Spain. It closed for good in 1990, with the first-floor bar still remembered as a lively spot for locals up until the end.

In January 2010, a few weeks before it was scheduled to be demolished, local resident Donnie McLean bought the property. Although the solid masonry walls were structurally sound and intact, the building was almost beyond repair. The wooden roof structure and most of the floor joists had caved in. The windows were gone.

"It was probably six months from being too far gone. I just couldn't stand to see it fall into complete ruin," says McLean.

It took him over 10 years, working largely by himself, but McLean has repaired the building to the point of making it stable and weathertight. A new roof, floor structure, and temporary replacement windows, salvaged from another local building, saved it from collapse. It is a remarkable, if not miraculous, feat by the friendly, unassuming Scotsman. He deflects any credit for what

he has done. "We just don't need to lose places like this," he says modestly in response to praise for the work he has done.

I have stayed many times at McLean's rental properties in Southend. He has frequently offered to give me a tour of the beautiful old building. In July 2024, I finally accepted his offer. Donnie, my son Jake, and I stood on the Keil Hotel roof, where residents once took their afternoon tea, and looked out over the water back to Dunaverty Rock and Northern Ireland beyond. "An old lady I knew said she remembered seeing the Lusitania sail past here on its way to Liverpool when she was a wee girl," he says wistfully.

The late afternoon wind buffeted the defiant structure as we all stood silently on the old roof, for what seemed like five minutes. As a registered architect for more than 30 years, I knew how much difficult, almost impossible, work that McLean put into saving this abandoned building. He did it because he values history.

History means something in Scotland. The past is alive in a way that is palpable and accessible. At Dunaverty, a 5,000-year-old standing stone sits between the 12th and 13th fairways. A burial cairn for the men, women and children of Clan MacDonald that were slaughtered in the Battle of Dunaverty in 1647 lies in a field not far from the 1st tee. The passage of time, while often cruel, and always inevitable, seems to move differently in Southend.

Scottish links evolve over time. Dunaverty is no exception. It was laid out in 1889 by the founding members. The 1st tee of the original layout was on the north side of the Conieglen River across from the present 15th tee and played to a green in the same vicinity as the current 14th green. Shortly after World War II, the holes on the west side of the river—on the Machribeg Farm land—were modified. This routing is what exists today.

The current clubhouse is the third one—built in 1970 and expanded several times since. If there is a friendlier place in golf, I have not found it. Everyone is welcome. The restaurant, The Putt Stop, is run by the wonderful Moyra Paterson and is popular with non-golfers. However, it is golfers—both members and visitors—that are given priority. The walls are adorned with the names of past captains and club champions—MacBraynes, MacVicars,

MacMillans and Watsons. The light-filled dining area looks out to the 18th green and 1st tee. Binoculars on the windowsill allow the progress of golfers on the horizon to be monitored. It is not uncommon to see the tiny silhouette of a three-ball game on the high 14th tee before 10 a.m. and hear someone announce to the room, "Look, Sandy, Za and Graeme are already on the 14th." Golf is played at a lively pace at Dunaverty. It never feels rushed.

Depending on the time of year, grazing cows from Machribeg Farm are liable to be your main hazard on the opening tee shot. The fairway is wide and parallel to the 18th. It is an unassuming, but deceptive, start. The approach shot into the elevated and exposed green is one of the trickiest on the course. The short 2nd hole plays towards a caravan park. The holes are fun, not overly taxing, and serve to ease the golfer into the wonders to come.

A short walk from the 2nd green to the 3rd tee, located high above the golden strand with the ghostly Keil looming beyond, starts a run of holes through the 13th that is unique in golf. The 4th hole, simply called Dunaverty, is played over a high dune ridge to a punchbowl green located in a hidden dell. It is the essence of Scottish golf distilled into 179 yards.

It is a generally accepted club legend that the great James Braid himself visited Dunaverty in the early 1900s and advised on the current location of the 4th green. Prolific local author and lifelong Dunaverty member Angus MacVicar recounted the story briefly in his classic 1983 book, *Golf in My Gallowses,* as well as in the club's centennial history he wrote in 1989. MacVicar recounts the story in such a way that it is obvious he believes it to be true. That is good enough for me. I will declare it as truth now:

> James Braid recommended the location of the 4th green at Dunaverty Golf Club.

About 50 yards from the 4th green, along the ancient sandy track to Dunaverty Rock, sits the Sea Captain's House and the Summer Cottage—two wonderful old Royal National Lifeboat Institution structures that Donnie McLean rents as holiday rental properties. The small, intricate buildings have become something of a symbol for Dunaverty and Southend. I have stayed there many times over the years.

Like the 3rd through the 8th at nearby Machrihanish, the 5th through the 13th at Dunaverty is Scottish links perfection. The ever-present wind seems to come from all directions, and the shots inspire creativity. You are likely to use almost every club in your bag, although you could play with four or five clubs and have just as much fun. A bench between the 4th green and 5th tee is a good spot to sit for a moment and contemplate the wonders of nature. Sanda Island, rising dramatically from the water, looks close enough to touch. On a clear morning, the Ailsa Craig is visible on the horizon. Dolphins will break the still, glassy surface of Brunerican Bay—swimming happily, speaking an esoteric language we can only hope to understand. It can be preternaturally quiet in the early hours of the day. There is a feeling of peaceful remoteness. A round at Dunaverty is a welcome antidote to the chaos of the modern world.

Par is 66 at Dunaverty. There are seven par threes and a single par five. In club competitions it is rare to see a score under 70.

Rounds usually take three hours or less. For me, it is the ultimate combination of fun, shot variety, and natural beauty. Shiskine, just a few miles across the water on Arran, is the closest comparison. It is no surprise that there is an annual match-play competition, the Kilbrannan Cup, between the two clubs.

The run of the 9th, 10th and 11th is my favorite three-hole stretch of holes in the world. This triumvirate, for me, is the apex of links golf. Birdies and eagles are just as likely to come as bogeys and double bogeys—or worse. A steep climb up the 9th fairway reveals another perfectly hidden punchbowl green nestled in the base of the dunes. I have played the course many times in the last 30 years, but the sense of delight and anticipation I feel when reaching the top of the hill has not diminished. If anything, it has only gotten stronger as I have grown older.

Mt. Zion, the short, sheer, 120-yard 10th, is a masterpiece of design. Out on this part of the course the wind may change by the second. The tee shot can require as little as a sand wedge; or as much as a choked-down driver. Any shot that lands short, even a foot short, of the putting surface, will be repelled out of hand. The wide but narrow, tilted, green is a surprisingly small target. I once watched my friend Todd Schuster hit seven shots from the same spot, as the ball slowly rolled back to his feet time after time— starting out with a wedge before finally banging a putter up the vertical slope. He ultimately settled for an untidy 10. It was like the futility of Sisyphus on the steep hills of Tarturus. A promising round of one-under suddenly exploded to six-over. That is Dunaverty. That is links golf.

For me, the 11th tee is the center of the mythical golf universe. It is all there in front of you—ancient Dunaverty Rock, the tumbling links dotted with flags, the bright blue Kilbrannan Sound, the stark white Keil Hotel in the distance. On a sunny day, you will see the coast of Northern Ireland. If you ever make it here, take five minutes and sit down on the special bench that I dedicated to the memory of my son Jordan—*rest and be thankful*. I will be forever grateful to the club for placing the bench in this sacred spot.

As we progress around this incomparable links, the Keil acts as a constant beacon on the horizon, beckoning golfers towards home. Though the seaside withdraws, the inward nine has a multitude of charms: the blind approach shot on the 12th, the 13th green nestled in the dunes, the second—or more likely third—shot over the Conieglen River, and the road, on the iconic 17th. Machribeg, the finishing hole, is a chance for a birdie. The green sits just a few steps from the clubhouse, under the watchful and knowing eye of the members.

The perfect end to a round at Dunaverty, for me, was always afternoon tea at Muneroy General Store and Licensed Tearoom, located just down the A842 from the clubhouse. Started by an Italian immigrant in the 1940s, it has been run by Frances Hill and her husband Ian since 1994. Frances is one of the great bakers of the world. She is a master. Muneroy Tearoom was her passion for over 30 years. She closed it, reluctantly, at the end of 2024.

Time seemed to be suspended inside the old tearoom. It could be 2024, 1994, or 1954. The warm, welcoming dining room was

always full of people, with laughter filling the space. For an hour or so, the constant division and strife of the outside world could be left at the door. People talked to each other; phone usage was discouraged. The young servers recited the substantial list of pastries and cakes from memory—Mint-Chocolate Sponge Cake, Lemon and Raspberry Sponge Cake, Toffee Meringues, Millionaire Brownies. If I had one meal to try to explain Scotland to someone who had never visited the country, a late afternoon lunch with tea and cake at Muneroy would be my choice.

When Jake and I returned to Scotland in July 2024, I planned an entire day so we would have at least two hours for late afternoon tea at Muneroy. We arrived at 2 p.m. after making the 45 mile drive from the ferry landing at Claonaig. The dining room was full, as usual, but Frances had kindly saved a small table for the two of us. I had heard rumors that the Hills were considering selling the store and retiring, but I did not want to contemplate a world without Muneroy, so I decided not to ask about it.

The mint-chocolate sponge cake we had that day was the work of a culinary genius, which Frances Hill most surely is. We took our time over the tea and cake. The late afternoon sunlight streaked through the large windows, highlighting the wonderful old woodwork. Pop music from the 1970s and 80s filled the air. There were no thoughts of elections, fake, manufactured political outrage, or wars. Jake was so happy that I did not want the meal to end.

We went into the general store area to settle our substantial bill, gathering several items to take to our cottage at Dunaverty Rock, including a postcard of the Keil that looked like it was left over from the 1960s. Muneroy was always a cash only business. I took out several 20-pound notes as we put down cans of Tennent's, orange Fanta and Cadbury chocolate bars. Frances had come out of the kitchen to see us off. She sold me a bottle of Coke at this very counter in 1994.

"I'm not taking your money, Jim," she said softly, with a smile.

I attempted to protest. Ian was standing next to the register and had seen this all before.

"You'll not win this argument, son, might as well accept that now."

Frances walked out from behind the counter and gave me a hug. She seemed a little emotional. I suddenly found myself feeling reflective. "Thank you for everything. Thanks for this place. I'll see you next year," I said hopefully. Her eyes were now filled with tears. "Yes, Jim. I hope so. Thanks for all your support. You and Robbie have been so great to support us." My friend Robbie Wilson and I had visited the tearoom together a few years earlier, with Frances giving us more takeaway treats than we could carry.

Back at home in Alabama several weeks later, David Mac-Brayne, a good friend from Campbeltown and Dunaverty member, sent me a photo with a real estate listing for the sale of Muneroy General Store. I immediately sent the image to Frances, asking, "Is this true?" She replied a few hours later in a direct, honest—and Scottish—way.

> "Good morning, Jim. Yes, it has been my life and my everything. I love what I do and all the lovely friends I have made, but it's all we do seven days a week. I feel weary. It was a huge decision for us. I will keep in touch."

I felt a jolt of emotion as I recalled all the times I had been in that store over the years. I thought back to that first trip in 1994 when a young Frances Hill got annoyed with a young American tourist for paying for a Coke with a 20-pound note. Time just gets away from us all. I hope someone buys Muneroy and keeps it open as a store and tearoom—but it will never be the same without Frances. When I sent my friend Jamie Darling of *The Links Diary* the photo of the impending sale, he replied simply, "This is very sad news. How can you follow a master?"

Several years ago, Donnie MacLean lovingly restored the old lifeboat station and small outbuilding at Dunaverty Rock. A third building, the old boathouse, is his workshop/office. It cantilevers precipitously over Dunaverty Bay. The festive red roof installed by MacLean on the old structure is the perfect aesthetic for this spot. A jumbled interior contains a wild mélange of Scottish artifacts—old windows, doors, furniture, fishing and boating ephemera. A small desk with a computer is the only nod to the 21st century.

The lifeboat station was erected in 1867, a full 22 years before the first course was laid out for Dunaverty Golf Club. A tall, narrow stone structure, it appears as if it was built directly into Dunaverty Rock, which towers above it, the site of an ancient castle of Clan Donald. Iron rods tie the cut stone walls and chimney to the roof structure to combat the often-violent coastal winds. "The entire building just shakes sometimes in the winter," says MacLean.

Defying nature itself, the lifeboat station has stood intact for more than 150 years—an ongoing testament to the architect and the skill of local joiners and stonemasons. The arcane knowledge of the builders now seems ancient and mysterious, of another time that the world has forgotten. A carved stone plaque is laid into the tall gable end of the building:

> IN MEMORIAM
> JOHN RONALD KERR
> DROWNED
> ON THE
> 26th OCTOBER
> 1867
> IN HIS 22nd YEAR
> CHAS A. COOKE RIBA HON ARCH

Robert Kerr, a merchant from Lanarkshire, funded the construction of the lifeboat station in memory of his son who died while duck hunting in Kintyre. Every time I visit this sacred spot, I take a minute to reflect on this wonderful memorial from a father to a beloved son. I understand his pain. As humans we are not any different than people were in 1867.

On my last visit to Southend with Jake, we played golf in the morning with David MacBrayne, had lunch in the clubhouse at Moyra Paterson's wonderful café, then sat at Donnie MacLean's Summer Cottage watching the glorious sunset over Dunaverty Bay, and the Keil Hotel, until it was dark.

A round on the links of Dunaverty is a chiaroscuro of natural wonders. Every color on the spectrum will pass before your eyes as the clouds and sunlight shift across the landscape like a living Seurat painting. Greens, yellows, blues, purples, browns—light and dark. Pure links golf. Is there a better day to have than a morning round at Dunaverty with your son, followed by a long afternoon tea at Muneroy, and finishing with an evening sitting above the beach while the sun sets over Dunaverty Bay? For me, this is as good as it gets. With all due respect to the great Lou Reed, this is a perfect day.

Southend, Kintyre, with Sheep and Sanda Islands and Ailsa Craig beyond          21584

# 11

## Elie

# The Golf House Club

"We come to the links at Elie, not greatly celebrated
in golfing history, but deserving of fame both for their
intrinsic excellence and for the many good golfers of
which they have been the nursery."
—Horace Hutchinson, *The Badminton Library of Golf* (1890)

The legendary five-time Champion Golfer of The Year, and
golf course architect, James Braid was born in the village
of Earlsferry in 1870. It is believed that golf has been
played on the links of Elie, in Earlsferry, since the 16th century.
One of golf's greatest men learned to play the game here. While
the current routing is attributed to Old Tom Morris in 1895, it is
thought by some historians that Braid himself revised the links
in the 1920s, leaving us with the course that is played today. The
comprehensive 2021 biography, *Divine Fury of James Braid* by
George Payne, uncovered evidence that Braid clearly made several changes to his favorite links. This is not noted in the extensive *James Braid and his Four Hundred Golf Courses*, by John F.
Moreton and Ian Cumming. Whatever his level of involvement,
we must only look at just a few of Braid's fully credited commis-

sions—Brora, Panmure, Kilspindie, Millport, Stranraer, Boat of Garten, and St. Enodoc—to see the massive influence that Elie had on his design philosophy.

The Golf House Club at Elie is in the Kingdom of Fife, a mere five miles from Anstruther. Fife has so many great golf courses, in such a concentrated area, that it can be difficult for a visiting golfer to decide where to play. These decisions on which clubs to visit can seem monumental, because they are, as each day of a Scottish golf trip is precious. If you ever visit Fife, you must make time to play at Elie.

Elie has a unique collection of holes, 16 par fours and 2 par threes. It measures 6,233 yards with a par of 70. On the surface, such an assortment of holes might seem to be a recipe for monotonous golf. It is not. Elie is a sheer delight, from start to finish.

On my last visit in 2019, Jake and I arrived about an hour early for our 12:30 tee time. We were greeted warmly by then head professional Gavin Cook. The small, detached pro shop is the location of one of golf's great curiosities. A Royal Navy submarine periscope, salvaged from the HMS Excalibur in 1966, is mounted in the center and extends through the roof of the small, octagonal room. The periscope allows the staff to see if the fairway is clear beyond the hill over which the blind opening tee shot is played.

It was a Tuesday morning, and the course was not crowded. The friendly pro told us that we were free to go off, adding, "But I'm sure you'll be wanting some lunch first."

When playing golf in Scotland, I always recommend that you have lunch in the clubhouse, either before or after your round. We each had a ham and cheese toastie with potato-leek soup. It was, as with most things in Scottish clubhouses, simple, yet perfectly executed and beautifully presented. No meal is better than one enjoyed in anticipation of walking a great links.

A revealing incident occurred as I was paying for our meal at the kitchen window. The bill was not much, around £20 in total. The service was excellent. As I paid with a £20 note, I offered the steward a £5 tip. He quickly said, "Oh no, sir, that is way too much. I cannot accept that." A little confused, I asked, "How much should I give you?" "A pound will be sufficient, sir," he replied with a smile. Can you imagine this same scene occurring in an American clubhouse?

With lunch taken care of, and £4 richer for it, we returned to the Starter's Hut /Pro Shop. Gavin told us we were free to play away. It was an overcast day, but a very pleasant 60° F and relatively calm. The opening tee shot at Elie is an ideal example of one of the many things that is great about Scottish golf. I love blind shots. This singular golf pleasure occurs often at Elie, as blind shots occur with wonderful frequency. This 420-yard par-four 1st hole flawlessly sets the tone for what is to come. A constant 10-15 mph breeze, typical for a seaside links, was directly behind us as we started.

The 284-yard par-four 2nd hole plays back up the hill we just crossed and directly into the wind that had aided us on the 1st. Yardage is generally irrelevant in Scotland. This hole, a full 136 yards shorter than the one just completed, played at least two clubs longer. Upon reaching the elevated and fully exposed green, the entire wondrous scene of the links and village beyond unfolds in front of you. The ocean is in view from the gently rolling duneland for the next 15 holes. Like at the Old Course, there is a pleasant feeling of constant movement, of the progression of golfers in the distance, that is present at Elie. This is pure, elemental, Scottish links golf.

Deep bunkers guard the right and left flanks of the superb 3rd green, like Scylla and Charybdis. This downhill par three is as picturesque as any you can find, situated right on the edge of town. A word about the bunkers at Elie—they are deadly. You will likely be forced to play out sideways, or backwards, should you fall victim to one of these pits. The village, with all its charming Victorian structures, borders the left side of the hole. This spot, the 2nd green and 3rd tee at Elie, is one of the great places to be in golf. We stood there in respectful silence for a few seconds to take it all in. On a clear day, which this was decidedly not, it is possible to see across the Firth of Forth to North Berwick.

Approaching the 4th tee, golfers will notice a wee pub, The

19th Hole, just a few steps from the tee markers. On an increasingly cold and ominous looking day, the pub looked inviting. With no golfers in view behind us, we ducked in for a quick dram of whisky. The proprietor greeted us warmly and mentioned the approaching weather. She was not optimistic at the prospects. If the course is not crowded, you must stop for a quick visit. The 19th Hole Pub Elie should be a listed UNESCO World Heritage Site.

There is not a bad hole on this ethereal flowing linksland. The 4th and 5th holes continue the outward trek away from the clubhouse and lead to the 6th, which deserves special mention. It is a short par four at a seemingly insignificant 250 yards. The tee shot is completely blind, played over a ridge. If the hill is carried, the ball careens wildly towards a large, sloping green. The vast blue waters of the Firth of Forth suddenly appear, filling the horizon. There are a few deep bunkers to be avoided, all of which are at least a one stroke penalty. This hole demonstrates why the experience of true Scottish links golf cannot be truly replicated in other parts of the world, as much as a designer might hope to.

The 6th hole is where Jake and I became full converts to the Church of Elie. As we stood on the wild, undulating green, the clouds grew even more threatening. The wind began to gust to at least 35 mph. The temperature dropped suddenly, almost instan-

taneously. As the great Peter Alliss often said on the BBC golf coverage, "If you don't like the weather in Scotland, just wait a few minutes. It will change."

The routing of Elie is unusual and brilliant. Old Tom, in his wisdom, chose to take the 7th, 8th and 9th back inland, away from the sea, in a somewhat circular pattern. This can create totally different challenges from the wind direction; the type of spin needed for a proper shot may completely change. The weather was quickly deteriorating as we played this trio. The 7th, a short 241-yard, semi-blind par four is a particular favorite of this mini-loop.

At the end of this cunning inward journey lies another three-hole stretch, the 10th, 11th and 12th, that ranks with any three holes I have played. All the holes are hard by the sea, which has grown increasingly angry during our inland trek. The 10th is an ideal golf hole—280 yards, the tee shot blind over a rocky hill, to a gathering punchbowl green. This is the pure, unfiltered essence of links golf. It is one of Jake's favorite holes in Scotland.

The short 11th is the second and final par three at The Golf House Club. It is located hard by the beach. The wind coming off the Firth was now so strong that it was becoming difficult to stand. After we hit our tee shots, all Hell broke loose. A storm of Old Testament proportions came in off the North Sea. We finished the hole, playing it somewhat conventionally, but just barely. On the 12th tee, the rain was now blowing sideways at a shocking speed. It stung as it hit our faces. We saw a few other golfers concede to the weather and start making the long walk in. From the tee, even in this weather, it was obvious that the 12th is a great hole. "Should we go in, Dad?", Jake asked. I knew he did not want to give up on a round in Scotland. "Well, we are as from the clubhouse as you can get. We're out here and who knows when we'll be back. We might as well finish now. It might blow over," I said hopefully.

Unfortunately, the 12th proved to be our last semi-playable hole of the day. We both somehow contrived to make a bogey on the difficult and beautiful 434-yard, Cape-style par four. The green is near the rocky beach on the left and is framed by the tall headlands beyond. It completes one of the great three-hole stretches in the world. On the 13th tee, it simply became a survival test. The temperature dropped what felt like another 20 degrees, seemingly within seconds. At some point, if you make more than one trip to Scotland, you will be confronted at least once with the sudden onset of challenging conditions. The most expensive Gore-Tex waterproofs are useless in this type of weather. I have always tried to finish no matter how difficult it might be. I am so glad we kept going that day at Elie. More than six years later, it is something Jake and I still talk about frequently, with great affection. Experiences like this often become the most precious memories over time.

The remaining holes are, of course, all par fours. Visibility at this point was about 150 yards and our shots were being played along the ground. We were simply trying to advance the ball forward. I do recall playing the 303-yard 15th. For some reason, the now 40-mph gale shifted directly behind us, the rain briefly abated, and we were able to launch our tee shots into the stratosphere like a rocket. The drive is played blind, once more, over a tall dune ridge, which then feeds downhill to the green. It was yet another wonderful links golf hole—the only one of those final seven that we really were able to play in a conventional sense.

We managed to get through the 16th, which turned us right back into the face of the hurricane force winds that had aided us on the 15th. At this point, if the ball got more than three feet off the ground, it would be blown completely off the planet. I played the 17th with a choked down 7-iron, just hitting running half-chip shots about 60 yards at a time. It was so cold I could not feel my hands or feet. Jake and I looked at each other and started laughing. What else can you do?

It seemed that the conditions eased just slightly on the 18th, which is a lovely and elegant 340-yard par four. There are two strategically placed bunkers on the left-hand side at about 270 yards off the member's tee. We dutifully holed out and shook hands; our clothes completely soaked through. After grabbing a change of clothes from the car park, we went into the clubhouse to try to rejoin the world of humanity. A gentleman burst out in laughter upon seeing us enter the locker room. We must have been a sight indeed.

"You guys really finished? We saw you on the 11th. We walked in after the 9th. I am just now getting warm," he said incredulously.

He introduced himself as Martin from Yorkshire, up from England with a group of golf buddies to play all the great links of Fife. We commiserated over the weather, and he told me how much they had loved the first nine holes. "It is a great links," he said. I agreed and wished him well for the rest of his holiday. I am sure they still laugh about the crazy Americans that played in a hurricane at Elie.

When I was a golf-crazed kid growing up in Alabama, I dreamed of one day playing links golf in Scotland. In these dreams, I had an ideal vision of what Scottish links golf must be like, mainly formed from reading about golf and watching The Open Championship. The Golf House Club, Elie, is in some ways an ideal manifestation of these childhood dreams. It embodies so many things that are great about Scottish links golf.

Finally semi-warmed and dry, we returned to The 19th Hole Pub for the all-important recap of the round. Of all of golf's sacred rituals, this one is my favorite. It seems to take on an even greater significance after a round in Scotland. When the weather had first started looking ominous on the 6th fairway, our faithful photographer (Jake's then girlfriend) had wisely sought out the refuge of the pub. She was waiting for us there. As we sat down, the bartender looked at us and laughed, grabbing a bottle of Bowmore.

"You played golf in that shite? This one is on me."

# 12

## Golspie

# Stuck in the Middle

"Aye. I've been in a few wee things."
—Jimmy Yuill of Golspie

The upstairs clubhouse bar at Golspie is one of those places that just feels welcoming. It is the type of spot where you can sit in quiet reflection for an hour, perhaps nursing a pint, not realizing the time that has passed. There is no need to look at Instragram; a wall of glass inside the modern structure exposes a precious swath of linksland gently tumbling down to the Moray Firth. This rare strip of ground contains eight of the club's holes, altogether a fun, unusual conglomerate of linksland, heathland and parkland golf that owes much of its current layout to the assured hand of James Braid. Golspie Golf Club is located exactly halfway between Royal Dornoch and Brora, along the A9, in the historic county of Sunderland. Though it has often lived in the shadow of these two more well-known links, it should not.

A club's friendliness towards visitors is an important quality for me and Golspie is as welcoming a place as there is. One late morning in May 2022, while staying in the area for several days,

I was greeted in the bar by a lively gathering of club officers—Alasdair MacDougall, Ross Urquhart, Willam "Besh" MacBeath, Sheila Robertson, Jimmy Yuill, the then club president. Alasdair had kindly arranged an afternoon fourball match between Sheila and Ross against Jimmy and me. Of course, there was a general concern among the group that I first have my lunch. Within a few minutes, a bowl of lentil soup, with a cheese and onion toastie, had me sorted. Golspie is a *golf club* in the best sense of the term. It seems to be a large group of friends that simply enjoy spending time with each other, for all the many reasons this game appeals to us.

The match, if it can be called that, was great fun. It became clear after a few holes that Jimmy and I were way out of our depth. Sheila proved quickly to be a serious player, having been the Ladies Club Champion several times, and Ross never seemed to miss a shot. We were two down by the time we reached the 4th green.

Jimmy was a wonderful host. He showed me the old clubhouse across the road and explained that the green on the par-three 2nd hole used to be the 1st green. In the old days, prior to 1930, it was then approached from across the road where a row of houses now sits.

"You can see how the green is canted in that direction to receive shots. That is one reason the hole plays so tough now," said my partner.

While we walked down the 5th fairway, a brilliant short seaside par four called Sahara, I asked Jimmy if he lived in Golspie. "No, not full time. I travel quite a bit for my work," he replied. When I asked what that work might be, he replied, "I do a wee bit of acting, like."

James Evander Munro Yuill was born in the village of Golspie in 1956. As a student at The Royal Academy of Dramatic Art he met another young aspiring actor—Kenneth Branagh. They became lifelong friends. He had a small role in the 1983 Scottish cult classic *Local Hero* as the man who asks Mac (Peter Reigert) for his autograph near the end of the film. In 1988 he joined

Branagh's Renaissance Theatre Company and appeared in many productions including *Hamlet* and *Much Ado About Nothing*. Jimmy, as he is known to the world, went on to appear in several of Branagh's films. His list of television credits is extensive and is best known for playing the Detective Inspector Doug Kerson in the popular British series *Wycliffe*. Last year, I was watching the latest season of the BBC series *Shetland* when he suddenly appeared on screen as Angus Wallace, an obsessed conspiracy theorist who lives in a campervan near a secret research facility. I immediately yelled out, "Jimmy!," scaring my dog who was asleep on the couch.

At the time we played together, Jimmy was working with Branagh to get *A Haunting in Venice* produced, a third Hercule Poirot film. "I've also got a script I've been trying to get made," he said as we walked between shots, "It's about a journalist who sees a United States Senator kill his family. She moves to Golspie to hide out from people that are trying to kill her to keep her quiet." I asked if he would film it here. "Oh aye, that's the plan." If this film is ever produced, something tells me that Jimmy will include a golf scene at his home course.

There is a moment during a round at Golspie that is one of my favorites in golf. After the 5th, the course turns inland. The 6th

THE SUTHERLAND ARMS HOTEL. GOLSPIE. SUTHERLAND, SCOTLAND.

is a wonderful par three set in the dunes, followed by the equally good blind par-four 7th. Then the course suddenly transitions to pure heathland. The walk from the 7th green back to the 8th tee, through a sea of gorse and past an old signal bell, is an ideal passage. Holes 8 through 11 sit in the landscape perfectly, framed by heather and gorse, the obvious work of James Braid. It is a joy to play here—linksland to heathland to parkland and finally back to the linksland to finish. It is like the intricate plot of one of Jimmy Yuill's beloved Shakespearean plays.

We eventually lost 8&7 and played on to the 15th green, near the clubhouse, where we said our goodbyes. It is the most fun I've ever had getting demolished in a golf match. Alasdair appeared on the 16th tee, as if he had predicted the outcome, and joined me to play the last three holes, which are all wonderful—I ranked the par-three 16th as one of my top 100 holes in Scotland in *When Revelation Comes*.

In the summer of 2024, I brought Jake north to Golspie for the first time. We played another delightful round with Alasdair, this time joined by his good friend Besh. Jake played his usual lovely golf, and I struggled, losing ball after ball in the punishing rough. I apologized to our hosts for my poor play. "Don't be daft, Jim," said Alisdair. "We're having a good time. That's all that matters."

When Jake and I came down for dinner later that night at the Golspie Hotel, Besh was waiting for us at the front desk, holding a large Tesco bag full of golf balls.

"I feel bad that you lost so many balls today, Jim. Take these for the rest of your trip," he said, handing me a mixed bag of Titleist, Srixon, and Bridgestone balls.

It was such a thoughtful gesture; so typical of everything I have ever experienced at this special golf club. Maybe someday the world will get to see Golspie as Jimmy Yuill sees it.

# The Lost Golf Courses of Arran

"On their backs were vermiculite patterns that
were maps of the world in its becoming. Maps and
mazes. Of a thing which could not be put back.
Not be made right again. In the deep glens where
they lived all things were older than man and
they hummed of mystery."
—Cormac McCarthy, *The Road*

At one time in the early 1900s, it is generally accepted that
there were 11 golf courses on the 167 square mile Isle of
Arran, a natural golf paradise located between the coast
of Ayrshire and the Kintyre peninsula. With a population in 1910
of approximately 4,700, this equates to one golf course for every
427 people. In more geographical terms, there was a golf course
located roughly every five miles along the A841, which circles the
coastal perimeter of the island. The 1947 *Golfers Handbook* lists
only the following 10 courses: Brodick, Corrie, Corriecravie &
Sliddery, Kildonan, Lamlash, Lochranza, Machrie Bay, Pirnmill,

Shiskine, and Whiting Bay.

In the early 1900s there was also a course, and golf club, located at Lenamhor by Kilmory. It struggled to recover from the effects of World War I, like many British clubs, and was closed by the early 1930s. The Corriecravie and Pirnmill courses, though listed as still open in the 1947 guidebook, were all but abandoned following World War II—which also wreaked havoc on many of the smaller U.K. courses. Kildonan, by most accounts, continued to be open until as late as 1962, before closing to leave only the seven courses of Arran that exist today.

There is an argument to be made that this small island is the single greatest living museum of traditional Scottish golf courses. There is the Sacred Seven—Brodick, Corrie, Lamlash, Lochranza, Machrie Bay, Shiskine, and Whiting Bay—which are still largely the same as they were 100 years ago, although Lochranza has been converted to a fun 11-hole short course, perhaps with a wink to the 12 holes of Shiskine. These courses break almost every rule of modern golf course architecture. They are even more vibrant and fun because of it. Very few recollections remain extant for the lost courses of Arran, except a precious few octogenarian islanders who might vaguely recall the course at Kildonan. Though these places have now disappeared from living memory,

the land remains a silent testament to their existence. Pirnmill, Corriecravie, Lenamhor and Kildonan were stunning places to strike a golf ball—all glorious hillside, linksland, machair, and headland settings. A walk on these pastoral sites, amongst moss-covered granite boulders, winding burns, gorse and wind-stunted trees, is a form of time travel.

In April 2025, I was contacted by Karen Barbour of the Arran History Museum regarding the postcard collection of the late Arran historian Stuart Gough. We had previously corresponded regarding my search for information about the history of golf on the island.

"There may be some things hidden in there that would be of interest to you. Stuart had quite a nice collection," said Barbour, in the grand tradition of Scottish understatement.

Gough's wife Heather, a retired Arran High School English teacher, had generously granted me permission to use any part of the collection for this book. For three exciting hours I looked through a massive hoard of old black and white postcards dating from the 1890s to the 1950s. It proved to be a gold mine of information on the lost golf courses of Arran. Stuart was an obsessive collector. The postcards and ephemera were organized neatly by subject and village. There were photos that likely can be found nowhere in the world except this remarkable compendium.

A few days later, armed with several newly found photos, Jake and I set out with my friend Greg McCrae of Brodick, on a dreich morning—grey, misty and mysterious—to find the lost golf courses of Arran.

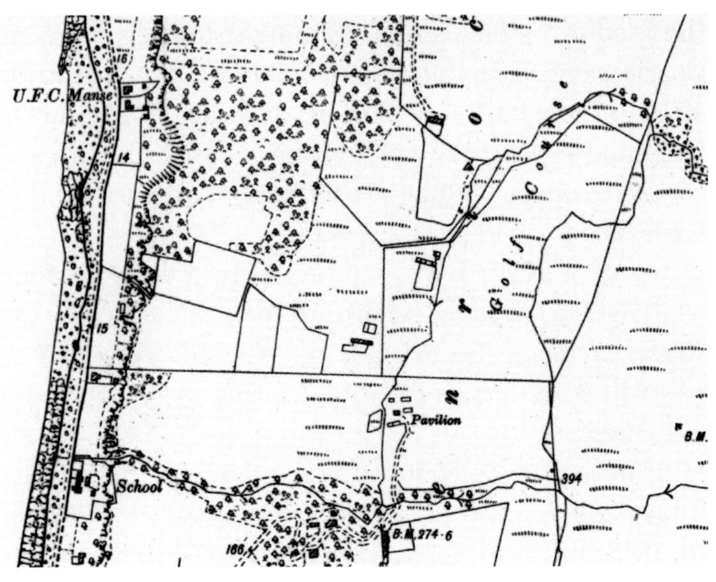

— — — PIRNMILL — — —

After a breakfast of sausage and scrambled eggs at the delight-ful Corrie Hotel, Greg met us outside the front door in his trusty Volkswagen Golf, an appropriate car for a man who has tirelessly and proudly promoted golf on Arran for the last several years. I first met him one evening in August 2021 in the Brodick Bar on the trip that became the basis for *When Revelation Comes*. He was walking home from the golf course—carrying his clubs- and stopped to buy me a pint of Tennent's. Three hours later we were friends and have been ever since.

"Good morning, gents! Ready for an adventure?", said McCrae as he stepped out of the small German car. The ominous looking sky and constant sound of lapping waves was a solemn counter-point to his preternatural cheerfulness.

Greg McCrae is the happiest, and most sincerely friendly, man I have ever met; his joy for living life is contagious. "We'll go to Pirnmill first, then continue to Corriecravie and Kildonan," he said as we all climbed into the Golf.

Lenamhor was not officially on our agenda, although we both had heard there might have once been a course there. (I had found nothing about it in Stuart Gough's extensive collection.) We turned left onto the A841, the Shore Road, passing through Sannox, over the mountain pass beside the rising slopes of Goatfell, before coming down through the lovely glen into Lochranza. The Lochranza course was shrouded in a light fog, though I could make out the statue-like form of a giant red deer in the mist. At the ferry terminal, just past the ruins of Lochranza Castle, cars and camper vans were queued up in anticipation of the 9:30 crossing to Claonaig. The normally calm Kilbrannan Sound looked somewhat forboding, even for the dependable *MV Catriona.*

As we progressed counterclockwise around the island, Pirnmill was the next village along the Shore Road. From the postcard photos and a rough hand drawn map found in the Gough Collection, we had a reasonable idea of where the course had been located. Despite this, in the best Scottish tradition, Greg stopped in at the Pirnmill Village Store and Post Office to ask for advice.

"Oh, aye, the course was just right the way up the hill. The old building there is still called the Golf House," said the friendly postmistress/shopkeeper.

The small shop was wonderful, packed with everything you could possibly need to enjoy a quiet Arran holiday—all arranged neatly and with pride. Thinking we might be in for a bit of walking, I grabbed an orange Lucozade and thanked the shop owner for her help.

The narrow, rough unpaved single-lane track wound up the hill from the village cluster of seaside cottages through lovely, wooded hillside farmland rising steeply into more open pasture land. Greg drove slowly and cautiously, especially for an islander. After two or three minutes the narrow lane passed closely between two houses. We were suddenly driving through someone's front garden. In the U.S. that is likely to get you attacked, but here an elderly woman stood in her doorway eyeing us curiously. Greg stopped the car to explain to her that we were looking for the old golf course.

"We don't get many cars up here. It's just a wee bit further. You'll see the old stone hut," the ancient looking Scot advised.

Just as she had proclaimed, we soon saw the ruins of an old stone bothy up ahead of us. The roadway, if it could be called that, abruptly ended. "I think we're on foot from here, boys," Greg said, shutting off the car. A narrow dirt footpath continued from the end of the road, transected by a clear, shallow burn dotted with smooth rocks. The creek was a fork from a much deeper burn on our left, lined with twisted, wind-stunted trees. The gray, misty haar was a bit thicker at this significantly higher elevation. If the three witches from Macbeth had suddenly appeared and delivered an arcane prophecy of doom, it would not have been a surprise.

It was a beautiful and mysterious landscape. We picked our way on the rocks, across the quickly moving stream, and emerged into an open, tumbling machair-like terrain dotted with large granite boulders. The simple stone building, its roof long gone, but walls and gable ends still intact, stood on our right between two curious small plateaus emerging from the hillside. We walked over to the structure, half hoping to find some long abandoned golfing relic.

The interior was only full of old farming detritus scattered among the collapsed wooden roof beams. No sign of golf.

We started south towards the sea. The terrain dipped down and then back up to reveal what must have been the Pirnmill golf course. Jake turned back towards the old golf house.

"That looks like it could've been two tees, Dad. Maybe it was the 1st and 18th," he observed.

Sure enough, without too much of a stretch of the imagination, you could picture the curious little plateaus as tees or greens—although much weathered over the course of 80 years. Climbing down the hill a little further, we soon lost sight of the bothy. The elusive sun emerged from the clouds, and the dramatic landscape was revealed in all its green, gray and violet glory. We were granted a vision of what it must have been like to play golf on this hillside, with a panoramic view of Kilbrannan Sound. From this spot, the churning sea seemed to take over the entire world. A quiet "damn" was all I said, almost to myself, as we silently took in the scene. A random philosophical thought came as the freshening breeze rushed over the three of us: this wind is the same as it was for the long-ago golfers of Pirnmill. Time, as the great Louisiana detective Russ Cohle once said, is a flat circle.

From this vantage point, it was easy to imagine the holes that ran back and forth across the slope; the smooth, springy turf interrupted by sheep or large outcroppings of weathered granite. Pirnmill must have been a glorious place to play this old game.

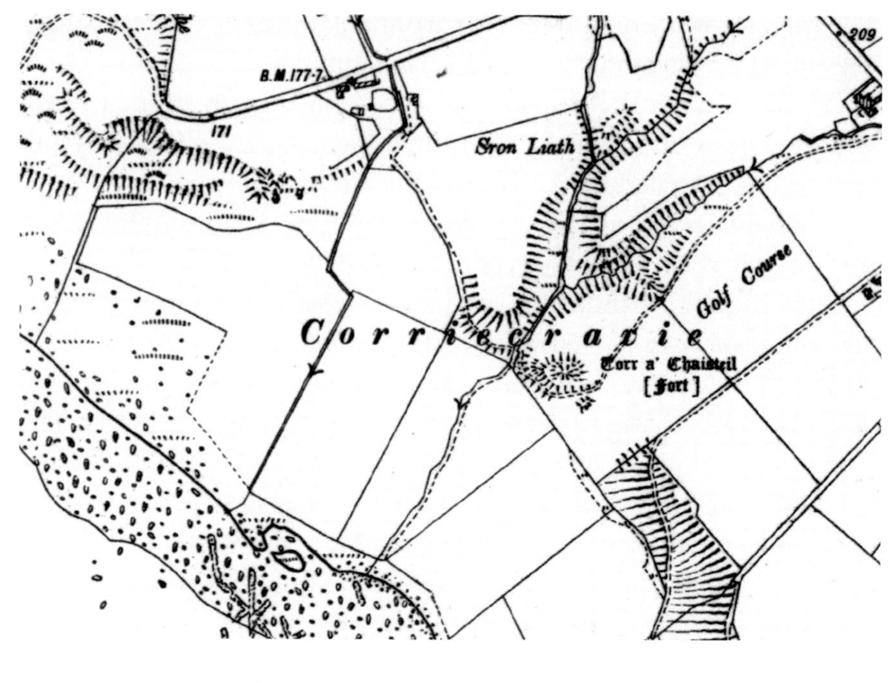

— — — **CORRIECRAVIE** — — —

The heavy, cold, mist returned as we walked back to Greg's car, picking our way back across the shallow, rock-filled stream. With the sun making only a brief appearance, the temperature seemed to drop 15 degrees in an instant. Soon we were back on the main road and driving through—quite literally—Machrie Bay Golf Club. This wonderful nine-hole course is the home of one of the most perfectly bizarre holes in Scotland, if not the world. The green on the par-four 9th hole sits between the A841 and the beach. A golfer must strike the semi-blind approach shot over the main road on Arran, listening to approaching vehicles to make sure the way is clear to play. The road winds on through Blackwaterfoot, the home of mythical Shiskine Golf and Tennis Club, before making a three mile climb to Corriecravie and Sliddery—the former site of the nine-hole Corriecravie Golf Club.

Just past the local fire station, about halfway to Sliddery, Greg pulled over to the side of the road near a cattle gate. The temperature had continued to plummet since we left Pirnmill and the wind was now blasting violently through the exposed gray-green landscape. "I think the course was just here—a wee bit down the hill," said our guide. The tumbling and varied terrain here is dramatic and dreamlike. It is likely the closest comparison to the magical linksland of Shiskine. No layout of the course exists, but a few photos from the Gough Collection showed that there was a small golf house and at least one or two holes down by the beach.

The land the course once occupied is now part of two different farms. On a nicer day we might have asked one of the farmers for permission to explore the property further. Scotland's "right to roam" law set forth on the 2003 Land Reform Act may have allowed us to enter, but common courtesy on private farmland supersedes that fantastic law. This course, which must have been a wonder, is now almost completely lost to the mists of time. The club never recovered from the forced shutdown during World War II. All that remains of Corriecravie Golf Club are a precious few black and white postcard images—the most striking one a group of men and women teeing off on the high 1st tee by the expanse of the sea. It is reminiscent of the medal tee on the 5th at nearby Shiskine. Imagination must suffice to envision the golfing paradise that Corriecravie must have been.

GOLF COURSE. CORRIECRAVIE

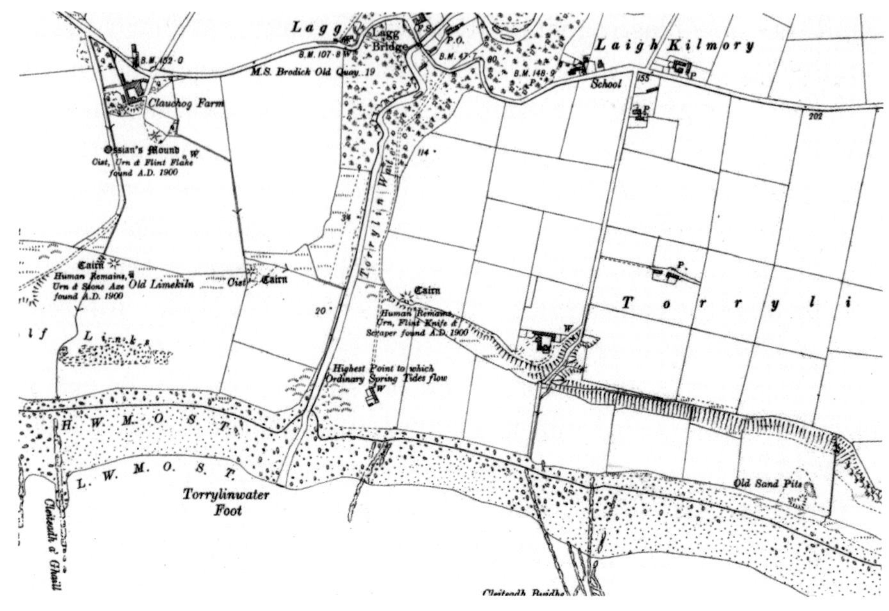


− − − **LENAMHOR (KILMORY)** − − −

Not far past Corriecravie and Sliddery the fantastically varied landscape of Arran changes once again. The land between the main road and the sea took on a gentler and machair-like aspect, sloping gradually down to the water. We stopped briefly at the strikingly modern Lagg Distillery hoping for a quick tour, but it was closed on Mondays. Just past Lagg, at Kilmory, Greg mentioned that he had heard vague rumors that there had once been a golf course here, too. We stopped briefly to look over the exposed farmland. A few months later the random factors aligned, and the magic of Arran would lead me to Lenamhor.

On the last night of this April 2025 trip, over pints in the Corrie Hotel, Greg tried to convince me to return in August to play for the Arran side in matches at Corrie and Shiskine organized by *The Links Diary*. When I realized this also coincided with the Kilbrannan Cup—a semi-annual match between Dunaverty and Shiskine—the wheels started turning. A quick call to David Mac-Brayne had me installed on the Dunaverty side, playing for my home course in Scotland. It would be a short trip for me—four days in Southend and four days in Corrie but one that I could not afford to miss.

The day before our island reconnaissance tour that spring, I spent a wondrous three hours in the Arran History Museum in historian Karen Barbour's office reviewing the Gough Collection. My wife had joined me for the return trip in August. There was a free morning before the Arran matches started at Corrie, so I took her into Brodick to hit all the shops—Wooley's Bakery, the Arran Chocolate Factory, the Cheese Shop, all the usual suspects. I was sitting on a bench by the beach, watching the new MV Glen Sannox sailing into Brodick, when a message from Karen Barbour appeared on my phone:

> "Heather Gough has found Stuart's postcard collection of the south end of the island. It's not part of the current museum collection. She said you are welcome to come to her house and look at it. Here's her number."

Excited at the prospect of finding new information, I immediately sent Heather a text message. She was busy with another meeting, but we found a 45-minute window that I could come by—leaving just enough time to still make it to Corrie for the golf. Her house was located on the road between Brodick and Corrie, just the way I would be going. The logistics fell seamlessly into place. Things always seem to work out on Arran.

When I arrived at Carlo, the lovely seaside cottage that she shared with her husband Stuart for over 30 years, a few ladies were leaving. They smiled and greeted me kindly as I walked past them on the road. I rang the bell and immediately heard "Come in, come in!" An older lady who was in the house, the last remnant of the just completed gathering, eyed me suspiciously before deciding I must be OK if the museum had sent me to look at old postcards.

Heather Gough, a small, energetic woman, welcomed me into her home like a long-lost friend. The large great room, with a high ceiling, was open to the kitchen. A thick leather album of postcards and random historical Arran ephemera was positioned on the kitchen table. Huge bay windows offered a panoramic view of the Firth, eerily calm on a windless morning.

"Coffee or tea for you, Jim?" she asked while sitting a plate of assorted biscuits next to the large green album.

I sat down and carefully opened the thick book that her husband had curated and collected for over 40 years. She brought the coffee, with a small pitcher of milk and a few packs of light brown sugar. I mentioned I had seen her late husband's collection a few months previously and that it was one of the most impressive, comprehensive caches of information I had ever seen.

"Oh, thank you. Stuart would have been so pleased to hear you say that. He spent years traveling and searching for any postcards related to Arran. It was his passion." There seemed to be tears forming in her eyes. I assumed that her husband's passing had been relatively recent. "I'll leave you to it, then," she said as she went into the next room.

Stuart Gough was a master. Like the previous collection, this one was organized neatly by location and village—Corriecravie, Kilmory, Kildonan, and Dippin. In addition to the postcards,

there were random map sketches and other items related to each small community—maybe an old hotel advertisement or a ticket to an important event at the village hall. I immediately noticed a few black and white images of the golf course at Corriecravie that I had never seen anywhere before. They probably only exist in this collection. It felt as if I was opening the Dead Sea Scrolls.

Kilmory was the next section in the book. Along with photos of the old Kilmory Hotel and other spectacular island vistas, there were two items that immediately stood out—one an image of a single, ancient Model T type car stopped on the main road, with a man in a suit standing beside it. It was titled *Cleats Golf Course, Kilmory*. On the next page was a receipt, dated June 22, 1911, for a members subscription fee of five shillings for Lenamhor Golf Club, Southend, Arran. I was in awe of these rare golf artifacts. In another part of the house, Heather Gough was singing a pleasant, lilting work song as she went about her daily tasks. There was not only a course at Kilmory, called Lenamhor, but it was an organized club. I later found the following news items that appeared in the daily *Ardrossan and Saltcoats Herald:*

> August 4, 1905
> Kilmory, Southend, Arran
> A meeting was held in the school on Saturday to form a golf club for the district. A committee was appointed, ground was obtained, and the course will be immediately laid out. The secretary is Mr. J. H. Duncan, Schoolhouse, Kilmory.

> April 20, 1906
> OPENING OF A NEW COURSE AT LENAMHOR, SOUTHEND, ARRAN
> On Saturday last this course of 18 holes, which is situated eight miles from Whiting Bay, was opened for play. The president of the club (Mr. Crawford, Lenamhor) gave a short account of the proceedings which led to the opening of the course. He then

introduced the Rev. A. W. Kennedy, parish minister, Kilmory, who declared the links open. He thereafter struck off the first ball and was joined by the president amidst applause. A silver-mounted golf club was presented to Rev. A. W. Kennedy. A competition for medals, open to all, was then engaged in. 22 players started. The result of the competition was as follows: Scratch Medal, Alan Kerr, Whiting Bay, 77.

I wonder if the silver-mounted golf club of Lenamhor still exists somewhere. It is somehow comforting to believe that it does.

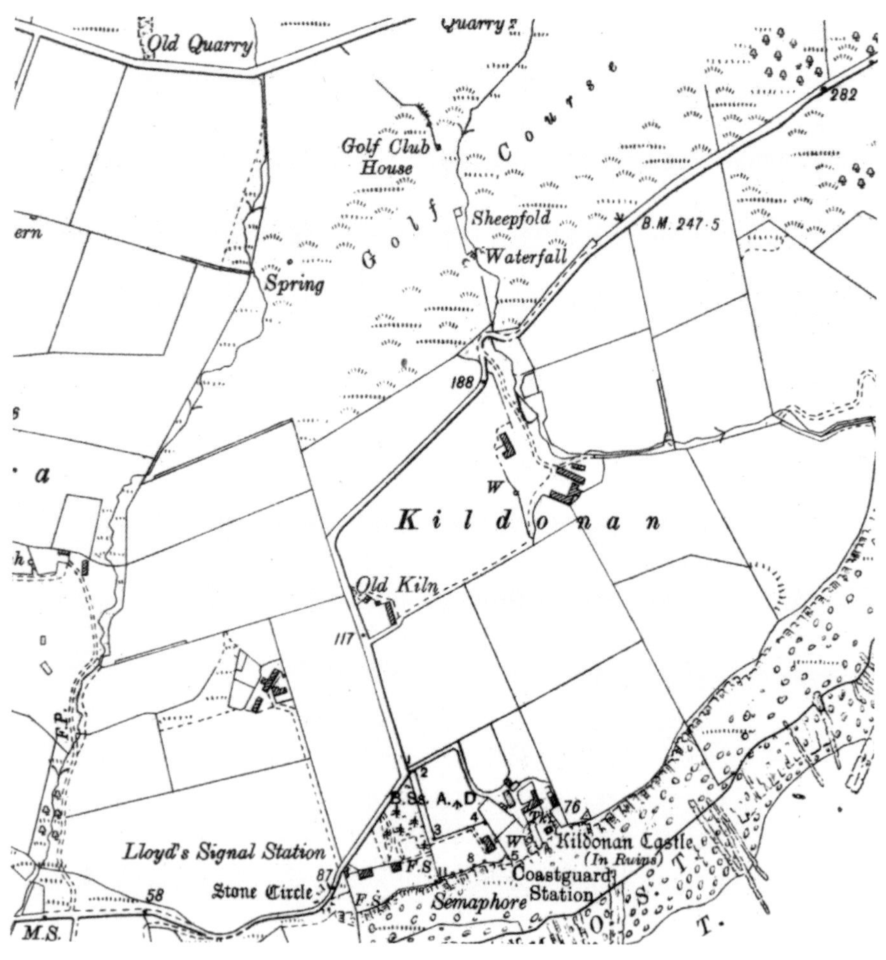

Another six miles along the Shore Road, just past the Pladda Lighthouse, lies the proud old village of Kildonan. It is divided into two sections—High Kildonan up on the headlands and Low Kildonan down by the sea, on a branch off the main road. The Kildonan Hotel, long a preferred destination for island visitors, is thought to date back as far as 1800. This would make it the oldest continually operating hotel on the island. From the 1890s until as late as 1960 there was a golf course in High Kildonan, near Dippin. It is mentioned in tourist brochures and guidebooks from the 1920s and 1930s, yet there is almost no physical evidence that the course ever existed. During my initial review in April 2025 of the Gough Collection at the Arran History Museum, there was not a single photo of the course, although there was a hand-drawn map showing the location of the course at the Dippin intersection of the A841. I had been on a nearly three-year quest to find photographic evidence of Kildonan Golf Club—looking through everything from the National Geographic archives to every old Arran tourist guidebook still in existence. There was nothing.

Armed with the crude but helpful map, Greg drove us to the spot where the course had been located. We walked to the bluebell shrouded fence to have a look. It is now lovely, open, cascading farmland sitting high above the sea. The views of Pladda and the Ailsa Craig were breathtaking. It is not difficult to envision a nine-hole golf course in this triangular piece of property. You can almost imagine where two or three of the green sites might have been tucked into corners. There may still be a few people left on Arran who remember the course, but their recollections have never been shared publicly.

Back to Carlo and the Gough kitchen a few months later, I felt a sense of nervous excitement as I turned to the last neatly labeled section, Kildonan and Dippin, in Stuart Gough's newly discovered volume. Finally, there it was—a creased black and white photo of happy men, women and children golfers holding bags with hickory shafted clubs. They were standing on a golf course, likely not far from where Greg, Jake and I had stood by the bluebells in April. A hastily scrawled note on the back read:

> April 1928. Kildonan. This was taken on Arran. Johnnie was away, he's not in it, but his wee niece is under me. Natives on one side—visitors on the other.

This is the only extant photo I know of, taken on the golf course at Kildonan. A course that existed for almost 70 years. Maybe someday a box of old photos will be discovered in the loft of the Kildonan Hotel, but for now this is all there is. It is a striking, beautiful photo and the people seem happy. Nothing has changed since 1928—the people you meet through this game are still the best thing about golf.

I had gotten completely lost in the past. My match at Corrie started in 15 minutes. Finding this 100-year-old photo had a strangely emotional and moving effect on me. Heather Gough's work song had stopped, and she suddenly appeared in the kitchen. Arran has its own sense of schedule—maybe she somehow knew it was time for me to leave. I started my goodbye.

"I cannot thank you enough for letting me do this, Heather.

Your husband was a master historian. I can tell how much he loved this island. I found a few more images that probably only exist on earth in this album. I'd like to use them in my new book, if that's ok. That's me. I've got to get to Corrie."

"Oh, I am so happy to hear this. Of course, you can use any of them you want—and you are welcome here anytime, Jim."

I have felt welcome on this extraordinary island, because of people like Heather Gough, for almost 30 years now.

Several weeks later, near the end of writing this book, I drove up to Nashville one evening to visit a trade show for the Golf Heritage Society. The exhibit floor was filled with displays of hickory clubs, balls, golf bags and old books—virtually every kind of historical golf ephemera. While perusing a shelf of ancient looking volumes, I picked up one titled *Nisbet's Golf Yearbook, 1911*. Like the more well-known *Golfers Handbook*, it contained an extensive listing of British courses of the day. On a whim I turned to the listing for the "K" courses and there it was, right after Kilbrittain and Kilburnie.

Kildonan Golf Club

Inst. 1907. Station—Whiting Bay. 3 miles. Hon. Sec.—Alex N. McNeil, Kildonan, Arran, Buteshire. Entrance Fee—Nil. Subs.—10s. 6d. ; Ladies, 7s. 6d.
Number of Holes—9. Terms for Visitors—1s. per day. (Ladies, 6d.), 3s. 6d. per week (Ladies, 2s. 6d.) ; 7s. 6d per month (Ladies 5s.) No Sunday play.

The turf, on soil naturally dry, is first class. The hazards are numerous, the holes vary from 180 to 430 yards in length. Magnificent views of the lower reaches of the Firth of Clyde. Service of brakes runs daily in connection with Railway Company Steamers, Whiting Bay.

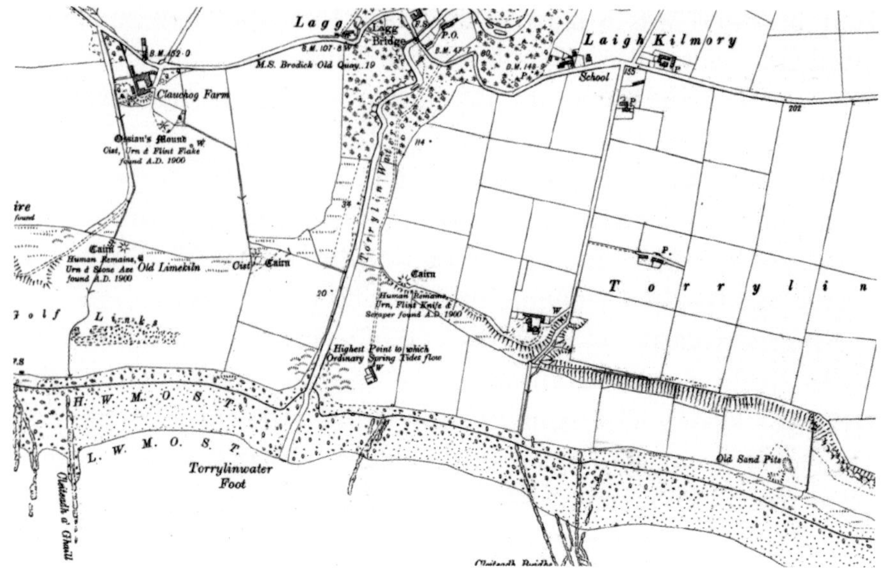


— — — LAGG — — —

It is generally known that there were 11 golf courses on Arran during the early 1900s. The golf boom of the late Victorian era swept over this tiny island like a tempest. Arran was a golf mecca in the age of paddle steamers and horse drawn coaches—maybe the first great golf holiday destination in the world.

During my final days of research for this book, I was studying the 1924 Ordnance Survey map of Arran available from the National Library of Scotland—and, sure enough, all 11 of those courses were noted on the beautiful hand-drawn map

While looking for the location of Corriecravie and Lenamhor, I noticed the words *"Golf Links"* on the beach just below a hill called Cnocan Faire—a few hundred yards from the site of the new Lagg Distillery. This course is not mentioned in any of the Arran guidebooks and brochures that I have collected over the years. It does not appear in any of the golf annuals of the day. There is no evidence of it in Stuart Gough's wonderful, comprehensive collection. Unlike even the scarcely known Lenamhor

Golf Club, there are no references to it in Scottish newspapers of the day. Yet, according to this beautiful old map, there was a golf links at Lagg. Having looked down on this spot from the hill above, it must have been an incredible place to strike a golf ball.

So, it appears, there were 12 golf courses on Arran in 1924. Seven of those remain. As golfers, in this age of slow rounds and usurious green fees, we are fortunate to still have Machrie Bay, Lochranza, Lamlash, Whiting Bay, Corrie and Shiskine, but we cannot forget the courses and people of Pirnmill, Corriecravie, Lenamhor, Kildonan—and Lagg. Those ancient golfers surely loved the game as much as we do. When the sun shone over the mountains of Arran, how glorious those lost golf courses must have been.

GOLF COURSE AND OLD MANSE, LOCH RANZA.

# 13

## Isle of Harris

## An Outer Hebrides Dream

"Islands do indeed possess strange and intriguing qualities. They lure you in with their uniqueness, captivating you with their history, people and folklore. And while lulling you with the pleasures of enticing isolation, they also spur the very spirit that brought you to them in the first place."
—David Yeadon, *Seasons on Harris*

On a cool and clear Sunday morning in May, the queue at Berneray Ferry Terminal was empty when my friend Robbie Wilson and I arrived from two wonderful days at Askernish. We had dutifully turned up about an hour early for the first sailing across the remote Sound of Harris. In fairness, we'd had our share of difficulties with Calmac, as we hopped from Oban to Mull to Iona to Skye to North Uist to South Uist to Eriskay to Berneray—and now we were about to cross over to the mythical Isle of Harris. The queue was empty. Satisfied that we would make the ferry without a problem, we set off on a futile search for a sausage roll and tea. A few minutes later we had completed a lovely tour of the tiny island of Berneray, but no breakfast was in hand. We walked to the edge of the slip to wait for the boat to arrive from Leverburgh.

There is golf and then there is ferry golf. Ferry golf is unmatched.

The crossing to the legendary Isle of Harris is about 45 minutes. Several cars had eventually joined the queue, and many people were now on the deck with us, most of them with dogs, ranging from English mastiffs to Scottish terriers. Dog watching is one of my favorite pastimes in Scotland.

There is a sense of anticipation and adventure when you take a ferry to play golf. A seasoned ferry traveler of more than 30 years, Robbie gave me his normal analysis of the condition of the boat. It was something I have grown to expect, and love, from him over the last few years. The small, older ship moved slowly, but steadily, across the dead calm, dangerously shallow, Sound of Harris. A series of large buoys marked the narrow channel that the ship must follow.

The Outer Hebrides of Scotland are a world treasure. I generally do not make statements about another country's government, because I am a visitor—but I hope that the Scottish government makes a concerted effort at some point to fully support and improve the CalMac ferry system. The islands and ferries are such a part of the national identity, it is sad that ships have been allowed to become outdated and there are no ready replacements, often causing numerous last-minute cancellations and delays. I have found, almost to a person, that the people who work for Caledonian MacBrayne are proud, helpful, sincere and do the best they can under sometimes impossible circumstances. The people of the islands deserve better.

We found a lovely food truck, the Butty Bus, just by the Leverburgh ferry terminal. It was still before noon, so there was no hurry to get to Isle of Harris Golf Club, which is located by Scarista Beach and was no more than 10 minutes away. A nice gentleman gave us the rundown of options to book our dinner reservation for the night, an important detail not to be overlooked.

At his suggestion, we settled on the Harris Hotel in Tarbert. I called and booked a table for two at 7:30.

There was a palpable sense of excitement as we got out of the car in the small car park at Isle of Harris Golf Club. Long-time golfers in Scotland can almost immediately sense when something special is laid out before them. Robbie walked over to get a view of the wonderfully cascading and rolling links that tumbled down to the ocean and beach below.

"I think you are going to love this, Jim."

One other car was parked next to ours. Two members were on the 1st tee warming up, just a few feet away. Robbie asked them how we should pay, and for some general directions regarding the layout. They were more than happy to advise us. We put our green fees in a small (unlocked) lock box in the unusual clubhouse, which is built into the side of a hill, like a house in The Shire from Tolkien's *The Lord of the Rings*. Everything about this place seemed perfect. An old, faded sign by the entry gate read "Golf Club Closed on Sundays." From what I have read about the Isle of Harris, I assume that it is advisable to make an appearance at the local kirk on Sunday morning.

Isle of Harris is an ideal example of why Scottish golf is a class of its own. The 267-yard, par-four 1st hole sets the tone brilliantly. It is thrillingly downhill, straight towards the vast blue sea, reminiscent of the opener at Isle of Skye or the 9th hole at Traigh—just pure golfing fun. I birdied the hole, which, of course, clouded my judgement. Despite my now unfair allegiances, the hole is an ideal opener.

The 299-yard, par-four 2nd hole, Scarista, is in my top 100 holes in Scotland. It is a Cape style hole, played around the ocean, to a perfectly located green that still makes me smile when I look back at the photos. Robbie and I stood on the tee for a few moments, both impressed with what was before us. I also birdied this one—playing a low running 8-iron from 120 yards off two dunes—which may make everything I write from this point forward subject to skepticism. This type of hole is one of the reasons that I love golf.

We climbed back up the very steep hill on the 3rd and eventually wound up back by the clubhouse and the 4th tee. The 145-yard, par-three 4th is also in my top 100 holes in Scotland. Forgive the hyperbole, but it is perfect. It is played, totally blind, to an aiming post about 100 yards aways. You hit and hope. Once over the ridge, we were confronted with one of the greatest views I have experienced on a golf course—the large punchbowl green, the links continuing into the valley beyond and Scarista Beach towered over by stark, greenish gray rocky hills. It is simply stunning. I won't attempt to describe it further, in hopes that you will make it there one day to form your own opinion. The vast, curving majestic beach and the remaining holes spread out before you like a pleasant dream.

Every one of the remaining holes ranges from good to great. The 486-yard, par-five 5th plays down through the dunes as if it has been there for 500 years. The wee 220-yard, par-four (!) 6th is just pure joy. The 349-yard, par-four 9th plays back up the hill to another great green site carved into the dunes. Every hole is fun and playable yet offers a distinct tactical challenge.

Earlier we had run into James, the greenskeeper, coming down the 5th fairway. He shut off his mower and before we even could say hello, he asked us sternly, "How did you pay your green fees?"

When he heard my American accent, I can only assume he was reassured that someone who would travel 3,500 miles to play golf at Isle of Harris would not cheat the club out of £20. Satisfied that our dues had been paid, we had a wonderful conversation about the course and his solitary efforts to maintain it.

The next morning, I got up at 6 a.m. and walked across the road from our bed and breakfast to play the 4th hole a few more times, this time with hickory clubs and an old Dunlop 65. When I was leaving, I saw James heading out towards the 5th hole riding his large mower. If he saw me, I hope my early morning golf was ok with him. It was a just sign of respect for Isle of Harris Golf Club—and the perfect 4th hole. I made sure to leave another £20 in the unlocked honesty box.

# 14

## Iona

# The Captain, the Crofter, the Mayor, and the Iona Open

"Road, stroll with me now
To the west-coast machair. Road,
Take my breath away."
—Robert Crawford, from *Icolmkill*

In October 1773, the famous duo of scientist Samuel Johnson and his faithful biographer James Boswell landed on the island of *I Chaluim Chille (Icolmkill),* the ancient Gaelic name of Iona, on their much-celebrated exploration of the Highlands and Western Islands of Scotland. Leaving Edinburgh in August, the pair started a circular trek up the northeast coast through Aberdeen, then west through the Highlands at Nairn, finally spending a large part of their expedition exploring much of the Inner Hebrides—Skye, Coll, Tiree, and Mull. Travel to these remote areas of Scotland was not easy in 1773. The Johnson-Boswell expedition felt like an exploration of a wild and largely unknown world. Even today, there is a feeling of isolation and remoteness as you navigate the length of Mull to reach the tiny village of Fionnphort and the short ferry across Iona Sound.

Iona has long held a near mythical place in the minds of many visitors to Scotland. It is remote and beautiful, which no doubt lends to its reputation. It is also pivotal in the story of Western religion; many travelers walk down the ferry slipway in almost reverential silence. A trip to Iona has the feeling of a pilgrimage, whether you are a believer or not.

Visitors are not allowed to bring cars on the tiny 4.5 square-mile island. Adventurous golfers, which one must be to enjoy the natural wonders of Iona Golf Course, carry their clubs onto the deck, sometimes through lapping seawater. This can create inquisitive stares from the often-serious pilgrims on their way to Iona Abbey, a holy site in the Christian religion. I have now made four trips to this special island. Each time some friendly pilgrim has said, incredulously, as we boarded the ferry, "There is a golf course on Iona?"

Yes, there is a golf course on Iona. One that embodies everything that is great and right about this ancient game. There is no clubhouse—the sole pub on the island, Martyrs Bay, acts as the unofficial gathering place. You will most likely have to walk more than a mile to reach the course from the ferry landing—although friendly locals are known to pick up hiking golfers along the single-lane track. When you arrive at the cattle gate entrance to the glorious machair, there is not even an honesty box for your green fees. Iona Golf Course is *free* to play for visitors. The vast Atlantic, a glowing neon blue shade that looks like the Caribbean, stretches into infinity beyond massive stone formations. Sheep graze idly near the 1st tee marker, oblivious to your presence. You could be forgiven for thinking the sandy road has ended at the gates of Heaven.

It is Thursday night before the annual Iona Open—held every second Friday in August for as long as anyone on the island can remember—and Finlay MacDonald is holding court in the wonderful Martyr's Bay Pub on the beach of Iona Sound. A few steps from the raucous gathering, just outside the bar, 68 Celtic Christian monks were slaughtered by marauding Vikings in 806 A.D. The mood inside is oblivious to the ancient atrocities. Finlay seems to know everyone, a mixture of locals and annual visitors here to play in the Open. Everyone certainly knows him.

Iona is embedded in MacDonald's DNA. His grandfather was an islander but left for the mainland for various reasons. He tore the roof off the old family home to avoid paying taxes on the property, per an obscure Scottish law. Eventually he became the captain of the first Caledonian MacBrayne car ferry from Oban to Craignure, so the sea is in Finlay's blood. Upon retirement, his grandparents returned to the island. They rebuilt the old family home place. MacDonald started playing in the Iona Open as a junior golfer. His summer school holidays were spent on the island with his grandparents. In 2012, he moved to Iona from Edinburgh. He asked his wife to marry him by the 11th green. Today he runs daily boat tours to the Isle of Staffa, a stunning volcanic basalt promontory six miles off the coast of Iona in the open Atlantic, inhabited by puffins and seals. Finlay MacDonald is a boat captain like his grandfather was.

The Staffa boat tours are finished every day by 3 p.m., so maintenance of the course largely falls to MacDonald, with help from one or two others. There are a multitude of challenges for the captain/greenskeeper, from a balky old mower, to marauding cows, to the harsh winter winds off the Atlantic:

> "You can't leave the flags out in the winter. They just
> get disintegrated. The wind on the west side of the
> island can average 35 miles an hour from the west or
> northwest in the winter. The flags just move so much
> that it shreds the material and then it bends the pins
> over and then it makes the holes bigger, which is good
> for our golf scores but it's not great for the course.

Also, the cows quite like to munch on the flags for some unknown reason. Once they bite them and chew through them, then the wind does the rest of the job. Look, we're very lucky out here. There have been clubs that donated things to us. I went onto a Facebook page last year and said, you know, what kind of flags do people use for windy conditions? And Stewart Fotheringham, the greenskeeper at Shiskine, sent me a box of sort of perforated ones."

MacDonald also serves as the unofficial tournament director for the annual Open. The few golfers on Iona have their own medal competitions, but the Open is the big event of the year—for the entire island. MacDonald religiously documents each year's results and scores. He makes the pairings, but players are encouraged to request specific partners if they wish. A naturally outgoing and friendly man, he is perfect for the role.

I first met Finlay a few years ago on the ferry from Oban to Craignure. He was on his way back from watching his beloved Glasgow Rangers play a big match against Eintracht Frankfurt in Spain. I had just posted a tweet mentioning that I was on my way to play Iona with my friend Robbie Wilson, when, almost immediately, I felt a tap on my shoulder.

"Are you Jim Hartsell? I follow you on Twitter. I just saw your tweet about Iona. I'm Finlay MacDonald and I'm a member there."

Finlay proceeded to describe the course to us in intricate detail, then offered to give us a ride to the course. Robbie and I were commanded to meet him for a pint in Martyr's Bay after our round. We have been friends ever since that day. He is that kind of person. His love for life and golf on Iona is contagious.

Saint Columba, who introduced Christian theology to Scotland, landed on the island of Iona in 563 AD. The Druids were there well before his arrival, having long understood the spiritual power of its stunning landscape. Golf came a bit later to the island. Allan MacBeth of Glasgow is believed to have laid out the original nine holes on the west side of the island in 1886. Around 1905, the course was extended to 18 holes onto Culbhuirg Farm by Professor McNeil Dixon of Glasgow University. The course lies on one of the rarest environments on earth, the machair, a fertile, sandy, low-lying grassy plain by the sea which exists in only a few places on the exposed west coasts of Scotland and Ireland. In 1934, a story on Iona in *The Scotsman* newspaper mentioned a golf course on the west shore of Iona "with turf second to none."

The Iona Open was revived in the 1960s, largely by a group of annual visitors from the mainland with ties to the island. They decided, ceremoniously, to call themselves The Honourable Company of Iona Golfers. A few years ago, a member of Muirfield—*The Honourable Company of Edinburgh Golfers*—played the course while on holiday on Iona. The rugged, completely natural links is the virtual antithesis of the near-perfect East Lothian course, but he loved it. An annual match was devised between the two Honourable Companies. Finlay has participated in it many times now. It is a day of foursomes held over the historic, serene links, with the full Muirfield experience. "It's just so much fun to play in the matches. The Muirfield members treat us so well. I even have to get out my coat and tie out of the closet," says the sea captain.

The discussion in the pub on the eve of the tournament veers wildly between the prospects for an upcoming Celtic and Rangers match and the pairings for the Open, which starts at 9 a.m. There are two other Americans in the eclectic crowd, as well as several of Finlay's college friends from the mainland. Finlay produces the pairings sheet, which is passed around to the raucous group.

Trowbridge Littleton, the mayor of the tiny town of Middleburg, Virginia, met Finlay in college while studying abroad in Scotland. Bridge, as he is known by all in attendance, has played in the Open 19 times and was named club captain in 2015. The captain presides over the annual prizegiving to the crowd, which gathers around the 11th green to cheer on the final groups. The Iona captaincy is an honor that Littleton considers one of the greatest in his life.

"That year, they replaced all the pin flags with embroidered U.S.A. flags saying 2015 Captain Bridge Littleton. They framed one of the pin flags for me and everybody signed it; it is in my house to this day. It meant so much to be embraced that way," says the mayor.

The annual trip to play in the Open is the highlight of Littleton's year. He loves the type of golf to be found on Iona. It is an antidote to the type of golf to be found in his own country.

"The golf course on Iona is like nothing I have ever come across in the world. It is laid out using the natural features and contours of the island in a way that makes it fun, challenging, breathtaking, and unique. What is most breathtaking is to walk from that 3rd green to the 4th tee box and see the wide vista of the island as it connects to the Irish Sea. It is like seeing heaven on earth. I think what is greatest about the course is that it is simply fun."

Bridge has only missed the Open twice since his first visit—once due to illness and the other time because of the Covid lockdown. His joy when discussing the event is poetic and uncontainable.

"The golf for the Open is simply the blank canvas upon which a truly unique and heartwarming experience is painted. It's an event that has a huge sense of tradition around community, friendship, and enjoying the company of wonderful people. For me, the open is not about the score, the cup, or even the wooden spoon, it's about belonging to something bigger and more important than yourself. It's about being embraced by a special community, focused on friendship, camaraderie, and good-natured fun."

It would be hard to imagine a more friendly, raucous gathering. It is after 9 p.m. and the pre-tournament party shows no signs of slowing down. Mindful of my early starting time, I slipped unnoticed out of the bar and made the short walk back to the Argyll Hotel. It was eerily quiet now in the orange-grey twilight. I could see the lights of Iona Abbey in the distance.

Outside the Argyll, the electric aquamarine blue of the Iona Sound glimmered like a sapphire on the morning of the Open. An older American, George Hilliard, who I had not seen at the pub the night before, was at breakfast at the table next to ours. When he learned I was playing in the Open, he put forth his entire history of coming to Iona. The event, and annual visit to Iona, had become the most important time of the year for him. After a full Scottish breakfast, I decided to walk to the course. Sheep standing in the roadway eyed me suspiciously, then sprinted away. Car after car stopped to offer me a ride, which I politely declined time and again. Finally, after about a mile into the walk, a van stopped.

"Who are you playing with today?" asks the friendly driver.

"John MacInnes," I reply.

"Oh, aye, you must be Jim Hartsell! John told me to pick you up if I saw you on the road."

Finally relenting to the hospitality, I threw my clubs in the back and climbed into the van with two other excited golfers.

It was a cool, clear, breezy morning on the ancient machair of Iona. Hopeful and excited golfers were everywhere. There was chipping and putting on the nearby 18th green and players trying

to warm up by hitting balls over the fence into Culbhuirg Farm; a croft farmed by the MacInnes family for six generations. Finlay MacDonald acts as the official Starter on the first tee, handing out scorecards and welcoming each player like an old friend. The format of the Open is simple and brilliant. Iona Golf Course has 18 holes, but the event has always been contested on only the first 11 holes—with each player throwing out their two worst holes for their official medal score. It is an ingenious handicap system. "The guys came up with this format in the 1960s. It was just easier than trying to give everyone a handicap, "says Finlay. "I don't have time for that. We also generally don't have time for 18 holes anyway. It's too much."

John MacInnes is the crofter who now runs Culbhuirg Farm. He has played in the Iona Open for 30 years. His brother Peter has come over from the mainland to make up our threesome for the day. Peter and John occasionally help MacDonald with course maintenance. Peter often cuts the greens when over on holiday from Glasgow. The brothers learned to play the game over the springy, perfect turf next to their childhood home. It was their playground, says John Macinnes.

"I spent hours and hours hacking around on the 8th and 9th with my brothers and friends. My grandparents were keen golfers, and we dug their clubs out one day and never looked back. We were so lucky to live on the course and have the freedom to go and play when we wanted to."

The conversation in our game flows freely and easily from the first shot. My decent opening drive, dead into a now stiff 20 mph breeze, is greeted with applause and shouts of encouragement. My hat flies off in the wind but is caught by someone behind the tee. The three of us walk together across a small burn which crosses the 1st fairway.

The 3rd hole at Iona is *sui generis*. It must be experienced to be fully understood. At 183 yards, it plays uphill over a massive natural blow-out bunker to a bowl-like plateau green situated at the base of enormous Archaean rock formations. The wind is blowing straight into us, but even on a calm day the hole is some sort of geographical oddity. It typically plays at least 100 yards longer than the yardage. A well-tracked drive still often leaves a full wedge or nine iron shot into the small, wildly sloping green. "It is unquestionably the greatest par threes in the world. A par on that hole is an eagle anywhere else," says Bridge Littleton. John made a great three, after a brilliant running chip, and I was thrilled to get a four. It is one of my favorite holes in golf.

John and I discussed life on Iona as we stood on the elevated tee of the wonderful 4th hole, a stunning par four that plays along the beach of *Camus Cuil an t-Saimh* (The Bay at the Back of the Ocean) and over a 40-foot-tall rock formation in the middle of the fairway. He is an eloquent, thoughtful man. I immediately sensed that being a crofter is not really work for him. It is something he simply loves doing every day. "We are really only custodians of the land for the short period of time we work on it, and I feel fortunate to have the opportunity to farm in a place like Iona," says the crofter. He loves his life here with his family and does not take any of it for granted. The generally temperate days of early summer are his favorite time on the island. "The days are long, and the season is full of hope. The dinghy is out so we can go fishing—maybe catch some lobsters if we're lucky—and then have a hack round the links in glorious conditions. It makes me really stop and take notice of my surroundings," says MacInnes.

There is a wonderful freedom that comes with playing the type of natural golf to be found at Iona. The internal pressure that often comes with putting is virtually nonexistent on the machair. "Just hit the ball straight at the hole, advises MacDonald, it will either go in or it won't." Bounces and hops on the primitive Iona greens are just as likely to cause the ball to go in the hole as to miss the extremely deep cups—necessitated by the wind and roaming cows. Rough is virtually nonexistent. The ever-present sheep see to that.

Putts are often accompanied by laughter at the result; whether good or bad. This ability to mentally let go of the outcome is strangely liberating. It also exposes an interesting comparison between the opposite spectrums of course conditions. In my experience, just as many putts seem to find the hole at Iona as might during a round at great Muirfield itself. At Iona, we seem to miraculously putt freely like we are twelve years old again. This is as close as any of us will ever get to experiencing the type of golf played by the Scots in the 1800s.

At the 7th hole we climb over the fence via a wooden stile and onto Culbhuirg Farm, on which Holes 8 through 16 are situated. The ground here is even more undulating and wild. The green sites are lovely and natural; situated in or behind rock formations or small natural dells. John, a fine player, makes an impossible up and down for par on the short par-three 9th. "A good short game is the key to playing well out here, Jim," he says with a smile. We can see his family's home from the green, a traditional Scottish farmhouse that looks inviting amongst the rocky grazing land.

The 10th and 11th holes at Iona are like something out of your wildest golfing dreams. On my previous two visits, the 10th fairway was filled with grazing sheep and cows. Today it is completely vacant. I can only assume that John had his loyal sheepdog round up the herd to keep them from interfering with the outcome of the Open. The 10th green is sited on a hill in the middle of several huge rocks. A narrow burn borders the right side of the fairway. The approach shot, played with a wedge today due to the now helping wind, is blind. It is simply a great hole.

There is an interesting debate among longtime members of the Honourable Company of Iona Golfers on how to mentally handle the unique Open format. When you reach the 10th tee, your nine-hole Open score is now the worst it can possibly be. This mentally frees up some players—and has the exact opposite effect on others. It is an interesting by-product of the singular format. The 11th hole is a dogleg-left par four, with the green situated in a natural bowl directly behind a rock structure that must be fifty feet tall. The green can only be reached from the tee by playing a huge draw around the rock and utilizing the natural contours of the ground. It is yet another one-off hole and sheer, unadulterated fun. For most golfers, it is a two-shot par four.

We holed our putts. I shook hands with my new friends, John

and Peter MacInnes. A crowd of spectators had gathered; families were having picnics on the rocks. Happy children and dogs were running around the machair. John finished with a brilliant 35 and was in contention for a spot in the coveted top three. Peter and I will not be anywhere near the prize podium, but that was irrelevant. We had just walked together for two hours, laughing at good and bad shots, in one of the most stunning spots on earth. That is the essence of golf. John grabbed each of us a tin of Tennent's and we toasted our good fortune for being together in this special place.

The penultimate group, which included Finlay MacDonald, reached the 11th green a few hours later. Finlay has played the round of his life. He has a putt for a 32 to tie the clubhouse lead of Neil Hill, father of Scottish golfer Calum Hill. Hill has shot his remarkable round playing with hickory clubs! In the steady 25 mph wind, that score may rank with Watson's final round 65 at Turnberry in 1977. The hole position on the 11th green is diabolical; on a steep slope near the back of the green.

After starting with a near miraculous 3-4-3 into the gale, Finlay had purposefully not kept up with his score. The pressure of the Open finally got to him, and he took three putts to finish. A few months later, Finlay was philosophical about his unfortunate finish:

> "I knew I was playing well, but I was playing with two
> friends who aren't from Iona that I don't get to play
> with very often, so I wasn't talking about scores at all.
> I hadn't kept up with it. I knew it was a good score, and
> I was playing well, but I deliberately wasn't counting
> it up. And then I did have a very bad 10th hole, I knew
> that, but I was like, it doesn't matter, I can score it off.
> On the 11th, I hit my drive, which I knew was on the
> green or thereabouts. I said to my mate, I said, I know
> I'm on a good score here, but I'm not counting because
> I've been told, don't count, because it puts you off
> your last couple holes. But then look at what I've just

done in the last hole there. It can't be any worse. And my mate Thumper said to me, he goes, do you want to know? I said, well, I can't really do any harm now. And he says, well, you're on the green and putting for 32-like. I was like, that just can't be right. He showed me the scorecard, and I was thinking, oh shit, yeah, I am. I'm actually putting for a 32! I knew that Neil Hill had made a 32 earlier in the day, because I'd been down to 11th and seen all the scores. And I was like, oh my God. Yeah, it's quite a psychological thing. What was most annoying about that was everybody kept saying, oh, you'll do it next year. I was like, no, there's almost no chance in Hell that I will play that well again on tournament day. Like I might play that well again sometime, but it won't be during the Open."

The crowd has grown in anticipation of the prizegiving and the captain's address. Roy Bowerman, an Englishman and this year's captain, hands out various prizes to juniors, women, and men. A large wooden spoon is given out annually to the highest score, to the loudest cheers of the day. Bowerman gave an eloquent and moving speech about how much Iona has meant to him over the years. He kindly mentions the detailed course guide I had made for the club to try to repay Finlay for the kindness shown on my two prior visits. A few signed copies of *When Revelation Comes* are included in the prizes. There are hugs all around as people say their goodbyes. In a long lifetime of playing in golf tournaments, the Iona Open is the most fun I have ever had in one.

Finlay invited my wife and I to his house for dinner before the annual ceilidh (a Scottish party with music, dancing, and storytelling) held in the lovely town hall after the Open. The scene inside MacDonald's beautiful home is like something from *The Big*

*Chill*. Several of his college mates, including Bridge, recap the events of the day—the good shots, the bad bounces, the golfing disasters, what might have been. The lament of golfers since the game began.

The food prepared by his wife Mairi is incredible; fresh local seafood and vegetables. It rivals any meal that I've ever had in Scotland. I sit quietly on the couch nursing a pint of Tennent's and listening to these happy friends talk about their college exploits, which no doubt grow each year in the telling. Finlay's two lovely, rambling children and the family's shy black Labrador add to the entertainment. The feeling of love in the room is palpable. I find myself getting a bit emotional at times, between the fits of unbridled laughter. It feels like an undeserved honor to have been welcomed so fully into such an intimate gathering. Finally, it's time to go to the town hall for the ceilidh. Mairi kindly offers to give us a ride in her car.

Everyone on the island appears to be packed into the town hall; a crisp, modern building with a great lighting and sound system. A golf-themed quiz night starts the celebration. Our table, which includes everyone from dinner, starts out strong. I help with the answer to an obscure golf question and feel like I just won the lottery. The group seems to just be getting started when we decide it is best to walk back to our hotel. The 7 a.m. ferry to Fionnphort is only a few hours away. We are sad to leave these lovely people, many of whom we only met a few hours earlier.

As we leave the ceilidh, with the music and dancing still going full blast, I see the crofter, John MacInnes, near the door. He puts a hand on my shoulder.

"I hope you'll come back again, Jim," he says as I shake his hand; yet another new friend that this wonderful country and golf has given me. I hope so too. Iona finds a place deep in your soul.

The ancient Gaelic monks prophesied that Iona would remain, even after the end of the world. If you ever walk on this ancient golfing ground, amongst John Macinnes' sheep and cows, you will leave hoping that their prophecy is true.

1st TEE AND CLUBHOUSE, MACHRIHANISH                    CL.4156

# 15

# Machrihanish

# Created by the Almighty and Old Tom

"Where do I begin to try to explain the joys of
   Machrihanish?"
—Michael Bamberger, *To the Linksland*

The first course I ever played in Scotland was Machrihanish. I was 26 years old. My dad and I stayed across the road on the 18th fairway at Ardell House, owned by the lovely David Baxter. We stayed there for a week. The view from Room #3 on the second floor was a golfer's dream—the sun setting a violent reddish orange over the mythical links each evening, with Islay floating in the shimmering Atlantic beyond. Every morning, the first thing I did was walk over to the large double-hung windows and stare at the breathtaking scene.

In the first group off the tee early one morning—armed with a £18 Day Ticket—I played 54 holes, only making a quick stop in the bar for a bowl of scotch broth and a cheese toastie. It was 7:30 in the evening when I finished the third round that day. My ever-patient dad, who had stopped playing after the first round, was waiting to greet me by the 18th green. There was still three hours of sunlight left. The incredible, almost unbelievable, links was deserted. As God is my holy witness, I would have gone around again if my dad had not asked if we could please go have dinner; last orders in the clubhouse were at 8 o'clock.

This was the day my love of Scottish golf, and Scotland, started to become a lifelong obsession. Playing all day at Machrihanish, alone on this great, hidden links, had been my road to Damascus experience. The next afternoon, Mr. Baxter convinced me to drive over to nearby Dunaverty to play—and that was it for me. I started checking into UK immigration requirements.

The bar and dining room in the wonderful old Machrihanish clubhouse, which was destroyed by fire in 2018, was a large open space with beautifully aged wood millwork and large bay windows. Not a bit tired after walking at least 20 miles, I ordered a Tennent's 70 Shilling. An old member at the bar asked me how I had got on. That's the way Machrihanish was back then. The few foreign visitors that made the trip all the way down the Kintyre Peninsula were welcomed like family. There was a sense of being sequestered from the world at a remote golf paradise.

The new, modern clubhouse is spectacular, but I miss the simplicity of the old days when the focus was mainly on golf and golfers. The course, despite its remoteness, is much more well known in the golf world now. People fly over to Kintyre in he-

licopters to avoid the winding three-and-a-half-hour drive from Glasgow. Gone are the days when a golf-obsessed American could consider skipping dinner to play 72 holes. All things change over time, but Machrihanish remains one of the world's greatest links. The circuitous, winding, drive from Glasgow is still the best three and a half hours that can be spent in a car. I advise skipping the helicopter and staying in Kintyre for a night or two.

Machrihanish has the most incomparable stretch of true links holes in the world.  The 3rd through the 8th is unmatched. It is wild, natural, impossibly rolling and tumbling linksland. Looking out from the tee to a tempestuous sea of rolling dunes and sand-hills can be overwhelming for the first time visitor. It can often be difficult to understand the best line of play—until the green is reached. Looking back towards the tee, the architectural genius of the Almighty and Old Tom Morris is fully revealed. The greens are among the most fun to play in Scotland, with steep slopes and severe drop-offs.

The back nine is often overlooked, but it is delightful. It generally plays straight into the prevailing wind. The land is not quite as dramatic, but the holes are fun and challenging. The 10th and 12th, both par fives, are truly great holes. The 15th green is a work of art; with its sheer left hand drop off. This is a course that everyone who loves links golf should play at least once in their lifetime.

Machrihanish is also where I first realized that the Scots are the culinary masters of the ancient art of making soup. I will never forget how good that Scotch broth was in the old Machrihanish clubhouse. It was in a large pot by the bar, and you served yourself. We ate it every day for lunch. My dad ate at least two bowls.

Those days near the Mull of Kintyre were brisk, if not cold, for two Americans from the deep south in Alabama. A bowl (or two) of scotch broth immediately banished the chill from a cold, windy, and sometimes wet morning round. When we got back home from that long ago trip, I looked up a few recipes and created my own version.

My dad is 81 years old now. To this day, I still occasionally take him his favorite meal: Scotch broth with a cheese and onion toastie. Without fail, he mentions that first trip to Machrihanish. I once heard the great Mississippi food writer John T. Edge say that recipes are a form of time travel. He is right.

SCOTCH BROTH
2 pounds lamb chops
4 quarts vegetable stock
½ cup pearl barley
1 white onion
2 turnips
6 carrots
3 leeks
¼ cup chopped parsley
Sea salt and white pepper

Place the lamb in a large stock pot and cover with vegetable stock. Bring to a boil and add the pearl barley. Simmer on low for about an hour and remove the meat. Skim off any fat. Slice the leeks (including some of the green tops), dice the carrots and turnips and add to the soup. Remove the meat from the bones and add to the soup. Season with salt and white pepper and simmer for another hour or so. Add finely chopped parsley in the last 15 minutes. Serve with an Arran cheddar and onion toastie.

After that first trip in 1994, I stayed with Mr. Baxter at Ardell House three more times. The trips sometimes included my uncle Charles and cousin Chris, both lifelong golf partners. David always treated us like family. He helped me join Machrihanish as a Country Member in 1996. At some point, life and work intervened. Traveling to Scotland was put on hold for only a few, but long, years. When I resumed regular visits to Kintyre, I stayed in Campbeltown, and then Southend. I wanted to be closer to Dunaverty. I lost touch with David Baxter.

In April 2023 the book launch party for *When Revelation Comes* was held in the Dunaverty clubhouse. It was one of the best days of my life. My friends Todd Schuster and Jim Sitar came over from the U.S. to attend, along with several Scottish friends—David and Ailie MacBrayne, Greg McCrae, Robbie Wilson, George and Anne Clark, William Paterson, and many members of Dunaverty. Scots are notorious for avoiding long drives. The fact that some of these people drove all the way down to the Mull of Kintyre meant more to me than I can ever express in words. The wonderful food was prepared by Moyra Paterson—a certain American golf personality ate about 12 of the meringues. It was a perfect afternoon.

I had just finished signing a few books when an elderly gentleman approached the table, accompanied by a much younger woman.

"Hello, Jim. Do you remember me?

"Yes, you're David Baxter."

It had been almost 25 years, but I knew him immediately. I walked around the table to shake his hand, which became more like an embrace. We talked for a few minutes, the years slipping away. Time is a flat circle.

David had been brought over to Dunaverty that afternoon by a friend. She approached me a few minutes later.

"Jim, David had seen that he was mentioned in your book. It meant so much to him. He lives alone now. His wife died several years ago and he closed the bed and breakfast. He remarried and then his 2nd wife passed away. My husband and I live in Machrihanish now and look after him a bit. We used to stay at Ardell House on our holidays. It means the world to him to see you again. Could you join us for tea at the Machrihanish clubhouse tomorrow?"

"Yes, of course," I said. It was the least I could do for the man who introduced me to Dunaverty.

We all met again the next day in the upstairs dining room at Machrihanish, the expansive wall of glass by our table revealing all the glory of the ancient linksland across the road. Golfers were teeing off on the mythical opening hole by the Atlantic, about to embark on one of life's great journeys. David, in his 80s now, seemed to remember everything from 30 years ago. If there is a consummate example of a gentleman, it is Mr. David Baxter. As I was leaving the table, he said, "Room three is always open for you, Jim. You can stay with me anytime."

"Upstairs, right by the wee bar," I replied.

"Yes, with a bottle of Springbank waiting for you," he said with a smile.

## Sui Generis:

## Returning to the Old Course After 20 Years

"About that course golfers so often change their
views. They come to pray, remain for a short
while to scoff, and then come back again
another time to pray forever."
—Bernard Darwin

The agent at Lufthansa Gate A23 was cold, unsympathetic and detached. After 22 hours of travel, my son Jake and I were near the front of the boarding queue for the last leg of our trip—a two-hour flight to Glasgow. We had been delayed at each stop but had somehow managed to navigate the dystopian nightmare of changing planes in Frankfurt Airport in less than 25 minutes—with a lengthy bus ride between terminals, running through the airport, to make our flight in time. Jake scanned his phone at the gate and started walking towards the plane.

"I'm sorry, Mr. Hartsell. There is a problem. United has booked both of you off this flight since you were not going to be here in time," she said with the emotion of a robot. For a moment, I did not understand what she was saying.

"What are you talking about?" I said numbly, "You just started boarding the plane and we are standing here with our tickets."

"You will both have to get out of the line, sir," came the equally cold response. After standing at the counter for 20 minutes with no further acknowledgement from a single member of the Lufthansa staff, we were finally told there were no more flights to Glasgow that day. "I'm sorry sir, you will have to take this up with United," without even so much as directions on where to go.

Suddenly I started thinking of what we were going to miss, not so much for myself, but for Jake. He was visibly upset, but his sense of humor was intact.

"This would be like Frodo and Sam getting all the way to Mount Doom and the Eagles grabbing them and taking them back to The Shire to start over," he said drily.

The day after our arrival we were scheduled to have lunch at the Royal & Ancient clubhouse, followed by a late afternoon round on the most famous course in the world. It was a meticulously planned, once-in-a-lifetime day that was suddenly slipping away. By some miracle, we found the United desk through all the mass confusion the labyrinthine design of this airport creates. The agent was friendly and helpful, stating it was Lufthansa that took us off the flight, not United. Glasgow, she said, was not an option—but there was a flight to Edinburgh in three hours that she just might be able to get us on. After a few frantic phone calls to rental car agencies, we took the Edinburgh flight. The chances of our bags arriving in Scotland after this fiasco seemed impossible. A few hours later we were finally in Scotland, and just as we were about to give up on our luggage, it appeared. It was the last to come off the conveyor belt. We had the all-important coats and ties for the R&A visit, and our trip was saved.

The two-hour drive from Edinburgh to Anstruther was relatively easy. It was Sunday evening, and the motorway traffic was light. I called The Bank Hotel from the road and asked if we could get food at 9 p.m., which they graciously agreed to do. We walked into the public bar just as Bob MacIntyre was holing his winning putt for the Scottish Open title. The pub was packed with jubilant Scots. In 10 minutes, our luggage was in the room, joining our golf bags that arrived a few days earlier. We took two pints of Tennent's to our dining room table. Out the large bay window, we could see the Firth of Forth in the distance. Suddenly the crowd in the bar erupted with a cheer that shook the hotel—Spain had just scored a goal to go up 2-1 over England in the European Cup. We laughed at the jubilant scene and the absurdity of the day. The nightmare of Frankfurt Airport was quickly forgotten. I was back home in Scotland—and with my son.

After breakfast the next morning, we made the short drive over to Anstruther Golf Club. It had been Jake's favorite course from our previous trip in 2019. We were not due at the Royal & Ancient clubhouse until 11:30. "Anster" was meant to have been our first round when we arrived. The empty course looked pristine in the cool morning mist. "I hate Lufthansa for stealing this place from us," Jake said sadly. There is a path along the beach and the wonderful, shared 1st and 9th fairways. Two elderly women were wading in the freezing surf. "Let's walk a few holes. The club won't care," I replied. A gentleman walking along the fairway with his black labrador smiled as we passed by, "Brave gals," he remarked, nodding towards the breaking waves.

The world had changed so much in the four years since our last visit together. As I climbed the hill to the 2nd green and saw the iconic granite war memorial, the memories of 2019 came streaming back. We played 45 holes of golf that day. "I could never walk that much now," I thought to myself. At lunch, Jake had asked me to call Lundin Links and cancel our afternoon tee time there. He was having too much fun to leave Anstruther.

The greenskeeper was mowing the fringe and waved at us as we crested the hill. "Let's walk over to The Rockies," Jake said. The par-three 5th hole at Anstruther defies description. It is something we had discussed so many times over the last few years when we dreamed of coming back here together—maybe with his two brothers joining us. We sat on a bench by the tee and listened to the waves for several minutes. Finally, Jake broke the pleasant silence.

"I wish we could play this hole."

Back at The Bank, we changed into our respectable lunch attire and started the 20-minute drive to St. Andrews. We arrived around 10:30; fortunate to find an empty spot in the visitor's clubhouse car park. Walking towards the R&A, we passed many excited golfers, along with The Himalayas and curious tourists eating ice cream cones. On the 1st fairway path, 1999 Champion Golfer of the Year Paul Lawrie hurried past us with a nod, pushing his own clubs on a trolley. With a few minutes to kill, we stood on the fence behind the 18th green to watch a few groups come in. The sky was a panorama of a Scottish golfer's dream, immense blue interrupted by only a few wisps of cloudy white.

Just over Grannie Clark's Wynd, which crosses the fairway, I noticed a golfer playing her approach shot. The ball flew beautifully low in the breeze, running up just over the Valley of Sin. I watched the player and caddie walk towards the green and something about this golfer seemed curiously familiar. As they got closer, I was sure it was a friend, Christy Longfield, a PGA teaching professional who I had played with a few times at Sweetens Cove in Tennessee. I knew Christy was in Scotland on a dream trip that had also been serving as preparation for the upcoming U.S. Senior Women's Open at Fox Chapel, which she had qualified for. I had no idea that she would be in St. Andrews the same day as us. As she came off the green, we embraced and marveled at the wonders of chance. What were the odds of us meeting at this exact time at The Old Course? The magic of St Andrews is real.

Our host for lunch, local golf historian and writer Roger McStravick, appeared promptly at the agreed upon time. He was joined by Peter Grunwell, the owner of the wonderful Fine Golf Books in St. Andrews. "I've donated quite a bit to your cause over the years," I said to the bookseller with a laugh. We entered golf's Holy of Holies through a vestibule on the north side of the building.

The tour we were given of this storied building ranks as one of the memorable experiences of my golfing life. Following coffee and a stimulating discussion on the importance of golf history in the Big Room, Roger treated us to the grand tour. Around every corner were priceless artifacts I had seen in books since I was a child—portraits of Old Tom and brave Freddie Tait, rare architectural drawings, ancient course layouts, silver medals and trophies. It was almost too much to take in. When we ascended the staircase to the Dining Room, I blurted out "Oh my God!" upon seeing the picture mounted on the wall of the stair landing, the original oil painting of the Great Triumvirate: Vardon, Taylor and Braid. I hope I did not embarrass our host.

The luncheon was wonderfully formal; the carrot and coriander soup a particular highlight. We said our goodbyes in the entry hall in front of Tommy Morris's championship belt. Our 5:20 tee time—the first "dark time" of the day—was still almost four hours away. On the walk back to the visitors' clubhouse to change into our golf clothes, we stopped at The Himalayas. It was absolutely jammed with people; happy families on holiday. "Let's come back and play this," Jake said. In 30 minutes, we had paid our green fee and were on the greatest putting course in golf and the home of The St. Andrews Ladies Putting Club. It had been 25 years since I had played it. The passing of time, if possible, has made it even more of a joy to play. Jake laughed the entire way around. We briefly considered another round but thought it was best to make our way towards the 1st tee.

At the starter's hut, I asked if there was any chance of getting two caddies. It was such a late starting time, but I wanted Jake to have the full Old Course experience. The Starter was friendly but not promising.

"It may be tough. We haven't had enough caddies all day, but I'll see what I can do for you."

Tents were already going into place for the upcoming Women's Open. I went off to find a discreet place to loosen my back, which was still recovering from the long hours of travel. Our very first shot of the trip was going to be on the 1st tee of The Old Course. Most golfers will never feel the pressure of trying to win the Open

Championship, but this feeling must be comparable.

At 5 p.m., we met our host for the round, David Connor. David works with the St Andrews Links Trust, the organization responsible for managing the golfing treasures in town—The Old, the New, Eden, Strathtyrum, Jubilee, Balgove, and Castle.

"Jim? So lovely to finally meet you. Let's get you sorted. I've got you and Jake signed on as visitors."

We settled our green fees and were soon joined by another gentleman, Alan Hocknell, from San Diego, who completed our four-ball game. As we exchanged standard pleasantries, Alan mentioned that he works for Titleist. As if on cue, two caddies, Layden and John, appeared by the teeing ground. Layden, an outgoing man from Dundee who caddies to supplement his lorry driving job, took Jake's bag. He immediately offered to take a photo of the two of us with the R&A clubhouse in the background.

As we waited, I thought back to 1994. My Dad and I had walked down North Street at 5 a.m., from 5 Pilmour Place, carrying our golf bags, spikes clattering on the stone sidewalk—a wonderful sound now lost to "progress" in equipment. Turning right at Golf Place by The Dunvegan, which had only just opened that summer, we joined the legendary queue. These were very different times. There was only one gentleman, another American, waiting in line. By 8:30, we were off with a two-ball game from California. It was a magical round. I shot 77 and my dad shot 76, making par off the road on 17 and birdie on 18 to beat me by a stroke. Many of the shots are still fresh in my memory. My father was so happy that day. He had dreamed of playing The Old his entire life. Now here I was with my son, exactly 30 years later to the month, older now than my dad was then. So much had occurred over the long decades, triumphs of life and tragedies beyond reckoning, yet here we were in this holy place. I was so thankful to be standing on this tee again.

Jake leaned over and whispered to me, "I'm nervous, dad." "Me too, I said, let's just get it airborne and down the fairway." Somehow, we both managed to hit decent shots into the widest fairway in golf—which is not nearly so wide when standing on the tee with the out of bounds fence hard down the right. "That's safe as houses," my caddie John declared as my running draw scurried towards the Swilcan Bridge. The ball rolls on the turf of The Old like at no other course. With the sun beaming down and the wind freshening, we started walking through history.

There is no point in exhaustively describing specific hole by hole details. Anyone reading this most likely knows The Old Course by heart. We quickly settled into the pleasant conversation of golfers anticipating one of the great, if not the greatest, experiences in the game. There were plenty of well-played holes. David and Alan were lovely players. The first seven holes were downwind and Jake and I both managed to make a few pars. The assortment of shots that can be played on The Old are as varied and entertaining as anything in golf. That is the thing that stands out the most to me about playing here again. Our entire group made pars on the 8th hole, leading to a moment of celebration.

On the 9th tee, Jake pulled out an ancient persimmon Mac-Gregor driver and hit a lovely boring shot that rolled forever. It made me proud that he would hit that old club on one of the most famous short par fours in the world—during maybe his one chance to play here. The experience is what matters to him. The overall score is irrelevant. Executing a tee shot just as The Old dictates, with the type of club that Tony Lema might have used in 1964 and then making a par—that is where the joy lies for him. It is the Scottish way of playing.

It took us quite a while to get through The Loop, Holes 7 through 11. On the 11th, I hung back from the group and stood on the tee as they walked away, wanting to absorb this incredible scene into my memory. A group of eight shadowy figures, four players with their caddies, stood on the 12th tee in silhouette. The sun was alarmingly low over the Eden Estuary. Finishing this round now seemed like the most important thing in life. I wanted it for Jake. I wanted him to be able to say in 30 years that he played The Old Course with his dad. He had hit a great shot onto the 11th green in the freshening wind. At that moment, I would've paid £500 for him to make that putt. Knowing my dad, he had probably felt the same way about me back in 1994. He narrowly missed, making a solid par on one of the most famous short holes in the world. The circular nature of time suddenly became clearer to me.

The Old Course exists outside the ubiquitous golf course rankings. There is no other place like it—it is *sui generis*—so I find it pointless to include it in my own list of favorites. This ancient linksland poses questions that seem impossible to answer, yet the solution is there if our mind is only open to possibilities.

There is a feeling of constant movement across the landscape, like a sailboat on the ocean in a steady wind. Figures move and advance in the distance, drawn towards the promise of town and a well-earned rest.

A round at The Old is a live drama that takes place over the course of a few precious hours. There is almost a feeling of being propelled forward by an unseen force. At this point, I should have been exhausted after a day of travel and not much sleep, but I barely felt tired at all. If anything, I had more energy than when we started.

The difficult 13th was playing straight into the wind. After a good drive, I hit a low, driving 5-iron to 25 feet. I hope to be around for many more years and hit a few more good shots in Scotland, but it is very possible that I will never surpass that strike. Almost as soon as it left the club, John said, "Shot." This is the highest compliment that can be paid by a Scottish caddie. From my own golf perspective, that is all I need to take from this day.

Jake was continuing to make lovely swings on the inward holes. He cleared Hell Bunker on his second shot on the 14th and made a par. I started to hang back more and watch him play.

The conversation with David, Alan, John and Layden was wonderful. I had not embarrassed myself with my golf, something that mattered more to me than I cared to admit. On the 16th, the reverie was broken when I hit a drive straight at the dreaded Principal's Nose. "Oh, God, no!" exclaimed John. I knew immediately where it had gone. The bunkers at The Old Course are a 1.5 stroke penalty or worse.

The ball was in a horrific spot. The only play was out backwards, but even that would require a full swing. It is a mystery to me, but somehow, I caught the ball flush with a sand wedge and—aided by the ever-increasing wind—it flew at least 150 yards back towards the tee. At this point, I thought about picking up and just walking to the 17th tee, but something made me take a long iron and go after the ball. By the time I reached it everyone else was already waiting on the green, now over 250 yards away. It was mildly embarrassing, but I did not want to quit. I hit a good recovery back down the fairway and caught back up with John at my ball. We were 75 yards out and John suggested a knock down wedge. "Give me the 8-iron. I'm running this up," I said. "Aye," said my caddie, with what seemed like a tinge of respect. My Titleist never left the ground, almost hitting the pin, and stopped six feet away. "If you make bogey after that crazy 2nd shot, I will tell this story for the next 10 years," said John with a laugh. The Old Course rewards perseverance.

The bogey putt was well struck, right in the center of the putter face, but it caught the edge of the hole and spun out. "Unlucky," said my patient caddie, but it did not matter to me. I have never been prouder of a double bogey.

As we stood on the 17th tee, the light was fading fast—everything was slowly becoming gray, as if the course was disappearing before us like an apparition. Despite the lateness of the hour, Layden once again offered to take our photo. I put my arm around my son. So much had happened to us in the last three years. We had lost his little brother, who he had loved so much and protected—who should have been standing with us now in this sacred spot. I felt myself getting emotional, but we still had two holes to go. I let the moment pass quickly and we hurried down the fairway. David, in an act of kindness, was now just walking in and not playing. He wanted us to be able to finish.

The Road Hole is simply the greatest par four in the world. I am not breaking any new literary ground by declaring this. Even after playing the hole several times, the sheer brilliance of the green and the Road Hole bunker still provide a unique thrill.

Jake and I had walked out onto this green five years ago at dusk and texted Jordan several photos. "Wow, the Road Hole!" was the almost immediate response from Alabama. The memory of that moment sent a jolt through my body. Even after three years, there are still times when losing a child shocks you to the point of numbness. These moments pass much more quickly now. I am not sure if that is good or bad. It just is.

It was nearly dark on the 18th tee. The light from the R&A and the windows along The Links Road were our main source of illumination. We teed off quickly, stopping to get the all-important photo on the Swilcan Bridge. I had one with my dad from 1994 and I wanted one with Jake. You might think it is a bit cliché to do it, but the sense of history is real.

I hooked my second shot left, between the 1st tee and the green. All the casual spectators from earlier were gone. It was almost 10 p.m. As John and I approached the ball, one of the greens staff walked quickly by, carrying something.

"How has your round been, sir?" he asked.

"Wonderful. Just perfect," I replied.

Everyone was standing on the green as I ran another 8-iron along the ground, past the Valley of Sin, and onto the putting surface. "Let's make this par, Jim," said John. I think it was the first time he used my name all day. I felt that he really wanted me to make it—and not just to enhance his tip.

The ancient, resolute, granite buildings around us have stood as a silent witness to the greatest moments in golf history—Braid in 1905, Jones in 1930, Nicklaus in 1978, Ballesteros in 1984. More importantly, in my mind, they had served as the backdrop for all the people of the world who had travelled to this holy place—parents and children, lifelong friends, solitary pilgrims and former Open champions out for a bounce game just because it is The Old Course. It transcends the reason for its purpose; a mere game invented by bored shepherds 600 years ago.

Jake narrowly missed a long putt and tapped in for bogey. My par putt looked good but went over the edge and ran three feet by. I reached down to pick it up and David said, "Putt this one out,

Jim, it's the 18th at St. Andrews." I marked the ball and turned away to look towards town.

"Jim, do you mind getting the flag for me?" said Alan unexpectedly.

"Why can't the caddie do it?" I thought to myself. As I grabbed the pin, I noticed some black handwriting on the flag:

I LOVE YOU DAD

I was momentarily confused, but then thought, 'This is so nice. They got Jake to sign a flag for me."

We shook hands all around and walked over to the pavilion to settle the fees with John and Layden. Everyone had seemed strangely emotional on the green. David walked up with the rolled-up flag, neatly placed in a plastic tube. "I wouldn't want this to get damaged on your trip around Scotland," he said. I noticed that he had tears in his eyes. "It was so great to play with both of you today. I wanted you to have this," he said, handing me the tube.

I sorted out my bag, looking for the car key and my wallet. Before walking back to the car park, I unrolled the flag to look at it again. It finally struck me what David Connor of the Links Trust had done. The flag was embossed with a small drawing Jordan had done for me when he was nine years old. I had come home from my long commute one day to find it placed on the laptop keyboard in my office. Realizing what it was, I said, "Jake, I can't believe this. We have to find David before he leaves."

Half-running towards the visitors' clubhouse, we passed the now silent Himalayas, its dramatic mounds dark and mysterious in the dull gray twilight. The echoes of the infectious laughter of happy children hung in the air. "I've missed him. He's probably left," I thought sadly.

We made it just in time. David was about to leave the nearly empty parking lot. He had just loaded his clubs and was getting in the car. I called out to him and hurried over. "David, I don't even know what to say, I didn't realize what the flag was until you had already left," I said as tears came to my eyes. I couldn't get out much more than that. My new friend, made through this wondrous old game, was crying as he embraced me.

"I've read your book, Jim. When I saw this drawing that a nine-year-old kid in Alabama made of St. Andrews, it just—I was drawing football players at that age. It really made me stop and think how much what we do here in St. Andrews means to the rest of the world. It made me realize how lucky I am to be here. God bless you and your family." We embraced again and through the tears promised to meet again in this ancient town, in this holy and sacred place, in the Kingdom of Fife.

Jake had taken my clubs, mercifully, and was waiting for me at our rental car. "I'm hungry, dad. Where can we eat?" he said quietly. It was now around a quarter past 10 p.m. and we had not eaten since our wonderful R&A lunch. It was way too late for The Dunvegan, too late for most places. "There are some chip shops in Anstruther. Let's go there and try to find something," I said, hoping to find any place still open. Twenty minutes later we were back at The Bank. The friendly bartender directed us to a place by the harbor called Dervish Takeaway. "I think they are open until 11," he said uncertainly.

The day had finally caught up with me, and I was exhausted. I could not keep up with Jake as he power-walked through the empty streets of town, intent on finding food. The wind and waves along Shore Street broke the preternatural silence. It was around 10:50 when I saw Jake approaching two men who appeared to be closing for the night. They eyed us suspiciously as we walked into the brightly lit shop. At this point, I was useless and sat down as Jake negotiated for food. Before he could even speak, one of the imposing Middle Eastern gentlemen said, "All we have left is Chicken Pakora or I can make a pizza." Jake replied, in a wisdom that belies his age, "Chicken Pakora would be great."

I gave my son enough cash for a £20 tip, knowing that it is way too much for a regular tip in this country. I was just so happy we had found some food and an orange Fanta. When Jake told the man to keep the £20, his mood suddenly changed. "Let me give you some chips, too," he said, filling two large takeaway containers. We thanked him and walked across the street to sit on a bench by the harbor. He locked the door behind us. Neither of us said anything as we attacked the Chicken Pakora and chips, which ranks with the best meals of my entire life. Finally, Jake broke the silence.

"This day was incredible, dad. Thank you for bringing me with you. I love you."

Take your dad, your mom, your son, your daughter, your best friend, or your faithful golf partner to St. Andrews and play The Old Course. Do not wait until the perfect time—for all the random factors of life to align. There will never be a perfect time. The random factors never align. If golf is an important part of your life, do it now, with somebody you love. The Old Course, this sacred, mysterious, wondrous and ancient strip of linksland, exists outside of time. It will continue for as long as this world exists. We will not.

Prestwick Golf Course.

# 16

## Prestwick

# The Himalayas

"Shot."
—Chris McBride, Prestwick caddie

Prestwick, the storied and ancient links on the Ayrshire coast of Scotland, hosted its 20th Open Championship in 1898. In those still early years of golf's greatest tournament, the contest was held over two 36-hole days. The great English amateur Harold Hilton, defending Champion Golfer of the Year, found himself tied with Willie Park Jr. for the 1st round lead after an opening 76. He began the 2nd round with a solid 4-3-5-4 start. At the Himalayas, the completely blind, 206-yard, 5th hole at Prestwick Golf Club, the great man became undone.

In the morning round, Hilton had played a mid-iron over the massive sand dune which guards the hole to a spot just short of the green, leaving an easy pitch to the flag. The wind had strengthened after lunch, and he now felt a driving mashie was needed. This was a club he seldom used. The ensuing tee shot came off too low and flew straight into the tall bent grass in the face of the tall sandy ridge. As Hilton recalled in 1908's *My Golfing Reminiscences*, he marked the ball on a specific clump of bent grass and was able to find it, which ultimately proved to be his undoing.

> "I carefully watched the particular bunch of bent grass that it struck, and to this day I wish I had not. Notwithstanding that I knew the exact locality of the ball, it took some time to find it, and had I not marked it carefully down I should almost to a certainty have lost it; that would have been much to my advantage, as I could have come back to the tee and played three, with the possibility of obtaining a five—a figure which, as events turned out, would have been sufficient to give me the championship."

After several attempts to extract the ball from the sandy waste area, he eventually finished with a disastrous 8. The terrible score was a shock, but he immediately went back to his usual steady golf and ultimately finished only two strokes behind Harry Vardon, who won the second of his record six Open titles. Hilton went on to win four British Amateurs and a United States Amateur, but never seriously challenged in the Open Championship again. He never denied Vardon's greatness, but begrudged him that 1898 trophy for the remainder of his days.

There are many great blind par threes in golf—the 5th at Lahinch, 7th at Shiskine, 4th at Dunaverty and 15th at Cruden Bay come easily to mind. The Himalayas hole at Prestwick is the blueprint for them all. Built on the "new" part of the course in 1882, when the layout was expanded from its original 12-hole routing by then professional Charles Hunter, it is the essence of golfing fun. The sense of anticipation that you feel climbing up the dune and approaching the green, after your caddie has exclaimed "Shot!", is the ultimate golf pleasure.

The famed Pow Burn, so much a factor on the 3rd and 4th holes, crosses unassumingly just a few yards in front of the tee. For the first time visitor, what greets you on the 5th can be a shock. It is a massive 30-foot-tall sand dune covered in deep bent grass. A row of famous Prestwick railway sleepers reinforces the crest of the dune. Individual boards are painted blue, white or green to indicate the line of play with the corresponding tee. One of the iconic red Prestwick hole markers specifies if the flag is in the front, middle or back. For the average golfer the hole can play as little as a 7-iron or as much as a full driver. Like all links courses, it is all dependent on the wind. The prevailing breeze is generally downwind off the ocean. The color-coded system on the bulkhead is remarkably accurate, but Prestwick should always be played with a caddie.

Chris McBride has caddied at Prestwick for more than 40 years. The Ayrshire native has made knowing the course his life's work. There is no other person alive who understands the subtle nuances of the great links better than Chris. He is characteristically direct when describing how to play the Himalayas hole:

> "Well, I mean, you've got the blue marker, and you've got the white marker. And if you're on the blue tee, it's over the blue, and if you're on the white, it's over the white, because there's a slight difference in the angles. That's basically it. Of course, you've also got the green marker for the ladies tee up on the right. You know that's pretty much how you do it. But the thing about 5 is, if the pin is in the back, you must make sure you have enough club to carry over the front right bunker. You don't mind missing the green on the right side above that bunker. If the pin is in the front, you've got to actually go for it, you know. You can miss right if the pin is in the back, but you can't miss anywhere if it's in the middle or the front."

The bunkers at Prestwick are expertly placed and, like many historic links courses, severely punishing. Along with the wind, they serve as the main defense for the course. There are four bunkers in a row situated along the left side of the 5th green. These are a bad enough place to be, but the old caddie is more wary of the single sand pit on the right.

"The one on the right is by far the worst of the five. It's the deepest by quite some way. If the pin is in the back, you must have enough club to take that right front right bunker out of play. You can take your chances in pitching and running from there or putting from the edge of the green."

Over the years, Chris has caddied for politicians, actors, athletes and many professional golfers. "I've seen it all on the 5th. Ben Crenshaw hit a full driver to four feet and made a two. That shot has always stood out to me." He treats celebrities the same way he treats the average visiting golfer. He just wants them to have fun. "What difference does the overall score make? If you make a par or birdie on the 5th or 17th hole at Prestwick, that's something you will never forget," he says.

A good friend from Alabama, John Allen, played Prestwick for the first time in 2024 in the company of McBride, something I had helped arrange. A man that is not easily impressed, Allen was blown away by the historic old links.

"The first four holes were so great, and I was just enjoying being there so much. I didn't realize what kind of hole the 5th was. I normally do a little research on the courses I'm going to play, but I wanted Prestwick to be totally fresh and new. It was a bit disorienting for a second, but then I saw that bulkhead at the top of the dune," he recalls with a laugh.

Allen was in Scotland for the first time in decades with a good friend, Michael Ray from Colorado, who had never played a blind hole before. "It was so much fun to see Mike's reaction on the tee—then we both flew it straight into the damn wall," he recalls with a laugh. Their sympathetic caddie encouraged them to play another ball. He wanted them to have a good memory of the Himalayas. Both men reached the green on their second attempt.

Blind holes are only blind once, an old golf maxim that Chris McBride often repeats to his players. Allen is the newest fan of golf's most famous blind hole. "I've played a few of them over the years, but it's just normal and accepted in Scotland. We don't really have them in the States. I love having something so different to play. I'm not sure I could ever play another one that would make me appreciate a blind hole more than that one did."

A good shot at the Himalayas at Prestwick, maybe even leading to a par, is a memory to be treasured for a lifetime. If you are ever fortunate enough to climb up the dune on this sacred hole after a solid strike, spare a moment to think about poor old Harold Hilton. As you ascend the crushed shell path, also take time to think about the great Harry Vardon, John Henry Taylor, James Braid, and even brave Freddie Tait. The sense of anticipation, and the weight of history, is what golfers have felt at Prestwick for over 150 years.

7TH GREEN GOLF COURSE, BLACKWATERFOOT.

# 17

## Shiskine

## The Perfect Hole
## on the Perfect Course

"Golf is meant to be fun."
—Greg McCrae, Shiskine member

Willie Kelso, an 81-year-old retired cow and sheep farmer from Corriecravie, is a 10-time club champion at Shiskine Golf & Tennis Club, the mythical 12-hole links on the west coast of the Isle of Arran. Willie's knowledge of Shiskine, and golf, is surpassed only by his deep understanding of cows—a subject on which he is an undisputed expert. In the spring of 2022, I played a memorable round at Shiskine with Willie, Hamish Bannantyne, another former club champion, and Robbie Wilson of Lochgilphead. The low, late afternoon sun cast the ethereal links in a dull amber glow as we played our friendly match.

A round with Willie Kelso is sure to be filled with great conversation. The topics that evening included the joys and challenges of island life, the correct way to play the devious Crow's Nest and the dangers of marauding cattle. We played quickly, which is the Shiskine way, but it never seemed we were in a hurry. There is a wonderful rhythm to a round of golf on this tumbling strip of rare linksland. Standing just above the beach on the tee of the blind par-three 7th hole, curiously called Himalays, Hamish suddenly asked the two visitors a seemingly serious question:

"What's your favorite hole at Shiskine, Jim?"

"The Shore Hole," I replied, without hesitation.

"Aye, that's the one," affirmed the great Willie Kelso.

The 266-yard 6th hole, called the Shore Hole for obvious reasons, was laid out by Willie Park when he redesigned and expanded the original nine-hole Willie Fernie layout to 12 holes in 1913. For me it is the perfect golf hole, challenging and fair for both low and high handicap players. There is equal opportunity to score an eagle 2 or a triple bogey 7.

I played the Shore Hole in April 2024 with local member Peter King in the Kilbrannan Cup, a semiannual match between the members of Shiskine and Dunaverty, my home Scottish club located just across the Kilbrannan Sound. King, a former art instructor and brilliant artist, moved to Arran full-time a few years ago following his retirement. He was a graduate of the famed Glasgow School of Art, whose building was designed by Charles Rennie Mackintosh. I asked King if he had realized how incredible the building was when he studied there 50 years earlier:

"No, I wouldn't have done, would I? I was 19 years old. You don't really appreciate anything at that age. A few years later I realized how special it was."

Golf, and painting, take up most of his time these days. His artwork is bold and stunning, landscapes painted in oil that are wondrous compositions of light and color capturing the essence of the natural beauty of Arran and Kintyre. On the 6th tee I asked him how to play the Shore Hole:

> "The big hitters will take a draw out over the fence and bring it back in, to land sort of between the 7th tee and the green, where it will funnel down to the hole. Normal players like us want to start a wee bit right of the marker pole on the hill in the distance.

It's a tight line. Anything that is even slightly left is going to end up in what we call 'the dunny'—which is not a good place to be."

Having been in the dunny many times over the past 30 years—often after hitting what appeared to be a fairway splitting drive—I can attest to its inhospitable nature. It is a deep fescue covered gully situated well below the rolling, tumbling fairway and the high gorse covered dune ridge that frames the left side of the hole. There is also heather and the occasional whin bush. You can usually find your ball and play it—Shiskine members have an uncanny knack for locating wayward golf balls—but the shot will be totally blind from a thick, uneven lie. Any stroke from the dunny that gets the ball back into play is an excellent result.

This brings us to the green. By my reckoning, it is quite simply one of the top green sites in the world. It is an almost perfect punchbowl, in a natural hollow at the base of heather and gorse covered dunes. Depending on the season, the scene is painted either deep purple or bright yellow. There are no other comparable colors in nature. Willie Park had the good sense to place a green where one was always meant to be.

The Shore Hole offers its greatest gift as a coda, like the last line of a great novel. From the front of the 8th tee, high above the 6th green, we are afforded one of the great views in golf—back down the entire length of the Shore Hole. This vista is on par with the 11th tee at Dunaverty or the 9th tee at Cruden Bay. A miracle of golf course routing, this spot has everything—all the colors of a Peter King painting imposed over the rarest terrain in golf, true linksland. Having played Shiskine more than 50 times now, I still always pause for a moment here and silently thank the arcane powers that this place exists.

A few days later while playing Shiskine again, I received a message from Stewart Fotheringham, the head greenskeeper since 1989 and an artist like Peter King, albeit one with a natural canvas of native plants and sandy dunes.

"Would you like to have one of our old tee boxes, Jim? I've got them in the shed," the message read.

My response was quick. "Yes. Can I have one for the Shore Hole?"

When we reached the 12th tee, located by the greenkeeping sheds, a bright yellow tee box was sitting outside the door. The faded white plaque read:

> 6
> Shore Hole
> 266 YDS
> PAR 4
> S.I. 3

It is one of the best gifts I have ever received.

A round of golf at Shiskine has a curiously medicinal effect. Even at my age, I never seem to be tired after playing there. If anything, I gain energy from walking that rare strip of linksland. Twelve is the perfect number of holes, as Todd Schuster once said, as many people have said, after playing there for the first time. Twelve holes at Shiskine never feels like less than a full round of golf. You will want to go back out again after lunch. It almost seems mandatory. A 24-hole day on the links at Blackwaterfoot, with lunch, is only equaled for me by a day spent at Dunaverty.

To witness the pure joy that my son, Jake, feels when we are at Shiskine together is something that rejuvenates my soul. It is his favorite course in the world. When life gets difficult, as it often does, I sometimes think about being there with him. There is a sense of happiness and peace that I feel when being on the Crow's Nest, beside mighty Drumadoon Point, with the world of Shiskine Golf and Tennis Club spread out below. It is like what I feel when standing on the 11th tee at Dunaverty. For me, it is the best physical evidence of the existence of a higher power, more than sitting in a church building listening to a sermon will ever be.

Shiskine is a natural cathedral of sea, sky and rock. Walking the links on a clear day with Jake and Greg McCrae, talking to Stewart Fotheringham for a minute or two about his work, hitting a few good shots, laughing at the inevitable bad ones, discussing the game over a pint in the Kinloch Hotel bar, this is the *summum bonum*, the highest good, that golf offers us.

GOLF CLUB HOUSE AND PIER, WHITING BAY, ISLE OF ARRAN
D 569

# 18

# Whiting Bay

# The Essence of Scottish Golf

I dreamt I saw the Arran hills again,
Heather, green woods, waves breaking on the shore,
An old farm kitchen with a grey stone floor;
The cattle in the fields, the stacks of peat;
Bracken and bramble blossom—oh, how sweet
—R.J. Maclennan, "Glasgow Evening News" (1925)

The 1947 *Golfer's Handbook* lists a remarkable 10 golf courses on the 167 square mile Isle of Arran, which rises dramatically, miraculously, out of the sea between Ayrshire and Kintyre on the west coast of Scotland. In fact, there were 11 courses. That is a staggering figure of one golf course for every 380 people. A Victorian era golf boom in the 1890s saw the creation of courses at Brodick, Corrie (Sannox), Corriecravie, Kildonan, Lamlash, Lochranza, Machrie Bay, Pirnmill, Shiskine, Lagg, and Whiting Bay. Today, seven of these courses remain. A strong case could be made that Arran is the small island golf capitol of the world, a compact mecca of all forms of traditional Scottish golf—linksland, machair, headland, glen and hillside.

In this same 1947 list of courses, it is noted that for each location, save Brodick, that there shall be "No Sunday play." Brodick, always the bastion of progressive thinking on Arran, allowed for "Sunday play after 1:30 p.m." At least, potentially, this allowed the minister of St. Bride's Church to complete his fire and brimstone sermon before the sinful golfers ran amok on the links. I am reminded of one of my favorite Scottish stories from Alister MacKenzie's *The Spirit of St Andrews*:

> "The Scots take three things seriously. Their golf, their religion, and their politics. A friend of mine once told me he was on a yacht in the Western Highlands. His host said to them, 'We must all go to church tomorrow.' There was a general chorus of protest. Why should they go to church? Couldn't they play golf instead? Their host answered, 'If we do not go to church the natives will look on us as absolute heathens and we won't be able to get any butter or milk or chickens, so, go we must.'
>
> Next day, when the minister saw these fifty or sixty English come into his kirk, he preached a sermon against the wickedness of the English and finished up by saying, 'An' so ma good freens, ye will all go to Hell, and when you are in Hell, you will all cry to the Lord and say 'Oh Lord, we never kent it was such a place like this and the Lord in his infinite mercy and wisdom will say, (thumping the pulpit) 'Well, you ken it noo!"

Whiting Bay is "only" 4,451 yards from the medal tees, which are reserved for competitions only. It plays to a par of 63. There are nine par threes and nine par fours—perfect golf symmetry. The absence of par fives is not detrimental; it is not even noticeable. In Dr. Robert Price's useful 1989 book, *Scotland's Golf Courses*, he is characteristically direct, and correct, in his assessment of golf on Arran, "The golf courses on the Island of Arran are notable for three reasons: their fine scenic setting, their low green fees and their accessibility to visitors", while in the very next sentence almost dismissing them as mere "holiday golf."

The term holiday golf has always bothered me, as it has been used over the years to somehow relegate places, like Whiting Bay or Dunaverty—courses with non-standard pars of 63 and 66—to some lesser category of the game. This is, and always has been, utter nonsense. While pure fun in the holiday sense, Whiting Bay is also a serious challenge. Having played the course a few times now, it might have the toughest/most fun collection of par threes in Scotland. Anyone that can get around in level figures has played a great round of golf.

Doreen Mainds and her husband Colin moved from Glasgow to Arran more than nine years ago, after his retirement. The family had been visiting their holiday home on the island for 30 years. After relocating, she opened the Tartan Tablet Company in Whiting Bay. She produces many variations of the ancient Scottish delicacy, a traditional sweet confection made from butter, sugar and condensed milk. Wonderful flavors such as Arran Malt Whisky, Eden Mill Gin, and White Chocolate are among the best. Do not ask me how I know that each of these choices are delicious.

In 2023 she was named the first female Captain in the club's

long 130-year history. During her two-year term she presided over a complete overhaul of the wonderful, quintessentially Scottish, Whiting Bay clubhouse, which was funded by a generous £60k bequest to the club. The clubhouse, sitting a mere 50 feet from the back of the 18th green, is as friendly and welcoming as any I have ever visited. The captain's stewardship of the unexpected windfall is to be applauded. The new renovations only serve to enhance what was already a special place.

The welcome afforded to visitors at Whiting Bay is second to none. David Hackett, the club steward for many years, is a former plaster and drywall contractor who chose a less stressful, if no less busy, career path. A visit to the club feels like being invited into someone's home for an evening meal. David serves excellent food, with a pint if desired, and as much pleasant conversation as you can handle. On a recent visit, he proudly showed me a lovely architectural rendering of the original course layout. Our discussion, of course, eventually turned to golf on the island. He was honest to a fault.

"There is so much great golf on Arran. I love Whiting Bay and play here when I'm able. I probably shouldn't say this, but Corrie is my favorite course to play on the island. Don't tell anybody I said that," he said with a laugh.

Time seems to slow down, in the best way, inside David's delightful bar and dining room. A couple of years ago, on my first visit to the club, I was paired with Captain Mainds in a friendly match against Jake and my good friend Greg McCrae, Arran's unofficial Golf Ambassador. Doreen, a fine 14 handicap, good-naturedly agreed to play off the yellow tees with us. It was largely due to her play that the match was in question all the way to the 18th hole. She was the perfect host and her love of the club is obvious.

Now to the course itself, a hillside wonder that seems to float above the shining Firth of Clyde. A wonderful 1933 holiday guidebook called *The Holiday Isle of Arran* is effusive in its praise of Whiting Bay:

"Think of it! Following the little white ball over a course that faces the widespread Firth of Clyde, an ocean highway, with the eternal sentinel, Ailsa Craig, rising from the deep, the distant Heads of Ayr, and the far Loch Ryan."

Curiously, Whiting Bay is the only course, out of the 10 (or 11) on the island at the time, to be singled out for special praise in the 200-page guidebook.

This is a hillside course. There can be no question about that. The opening hole, a 260 yard, severely uphill, par four plays more like 360 yards. Once this summit has been scaled, the reward is a view that you will never forget. The green is benched into the side of the slope, like many of the delightful and whimsical greens at Whiting Bay, and local knowledge would dictate playing the ball off the bank on your approach. After holing out, it is understandable if you pause for a moment and take in the spectacular scene below. The Firth stretches to infinity and offers the promise that only a round of golf in Scotland, in full view of the sea, can afford.

The par threes are unique to say the least. Wee is perhaps not a strong enough word to describe the green on the 3rd, appropriately called Wee Wullie. It is a 150-yard blind shot to a raised green about the size of a two-pound coin. I am still not sure how to play this hole other than to hit a perfect shot into a four-foot circle, which Greg McCrae did on the day of our match. Chipping and a strong short game are crucial around this course, many greens will be missed, even by low handicap players. The 4th, called Plateau, continues this theme. It is a wonderful 83-yard hole, semi-blind to a slightly larger plateau green that severely punishes a left miss. The greens at Whiting Bay are wild and fun.

Having played golf in Scotland since 1994, I continue to be amazed at the insane variety and one-off nature of the holes just waiting to be discovered. The 8th hole at Whiting Bay immediately found a place in my top 100 holes in Scotland. To be honest, I do not want to describe it in detail so the same sense of wonder and discovery can be preserved for future visitors. It is a brilliant golf hole and one of the best I have played anywhere.

The remaining collection of par fours deserves nearly as much praise, especially the trio of the 12th, 14th and 15th. These holes are perfect examples of the wonders of Scottish golf. There are blind shots. There are infinity greens. You might putt your ball from 80 yards away. You might chip an 8-iron from 150 yards. You are almost certain to smile while playing this magnificent triumvirate. After hitting a putt from 90 yards on the 15th that rolled inexorably down the fairway and stopped 15 feet from the hole, Jake told me quietly as we walked to the next tee, "I love this hole, it's just incredible." The panoramic view of the glorious firth no doubt influenced his verdict, but it is a great hole.

I have mentioned that the greens at Whiting Bay are unique. The green on the uphill 121-yard 17th is like a Pink Floyd—Syd Barrett era—psychedelic odyssey of the mind. It's just pure madness and defies conventional description. It is difficult for photos to do proper justice. It is a rare example of reality defying the imagination.

The wildly downhill 383-yard 18th, 433 yards from the spectacular medal tee, has everything a finishing hole needs—dra-

ma, strategy, and stunning scenery. Due to the clubhouse location, many courses end on a much lower note than the course may deserve—not Whiting Bay. The clubhouse patio abuts the green, with the building itself sitting so close as to influence the approach. Like the clubhouses at Troon or Lytham, it is just a few steps away. One can only imagine the excitement when a hotly contested match reaches the final hole, and the patio is full of curious spectators.

Back in the clubhouse, David Hackett is always ready with lentil soup and a toastie. A pint is welcome, and restorative, after this wild ramble above the sea. The talk quickly turns to the just completed match. The outcome may be mentioned briefly, but the individual shots are what take precedence in the conversation—a brilliant running chip on the 17th, a drive over the hill on the 12th that found just the right landing spot and ran down to the green, a hooked 3-wood over the heather and gorse on the 8th that miraculously found the putting surface.

It has always been this way on Arran. The old *Holiday Isle of Arran* guide sums it up wonderfully:

> "And the golf clubhouse at Whiting Bay, the dining rooms at Brodick, Lamlash and Lochranza, can be animate with conversation on the day's play on the island or at some professional or international tourney over the water at Turnberry, or far away at Gleneagles, or Carnoustie or Westward Ho!"

A round of golf at Whiting Bay, on magnificent Arran—with its peaceful glens, clear lochs, spectacular mountains and rolling linksland—followed by a late afternoon lunch of fresh scallops at Mara Fish House, finished with a piece of Doreen Mainds' white chocolate tablet for dessert and a wee dram (or two) of Arran whisky in the Corrie Hotel bar to end the day. What else do you need from a day of golf? What else could you need from a day?

Golf Course and Holy Isle, Whiting Bay, Arran

# CODA - THE 19TH HOLE

## Other Scottish Favorites

"It looked good from the road, but all golf courses look good from the road."
—Jake Hartsell

I have played 108 courses in Scotland since 1994. It was a challenge to pick only 18 favorites. There are so many courses I love and where I have been so warmly welcomed over the years. Here are a few special places that just missed the cut.

### Durness

Remote, raw, and stunning. The concerted effort it takes to get there is repaid ten-fold. As much as any place I have ever played, the sense of complete isolation from the rest of the world is almost overwhelming. This is a good thing.

### North Berwick

An East Coast cousin of Prestwick. Historic, quirky and fun in all the best ways. The skyrocketing visitor green fees make me sad, but that's the reality of the world. If you only have one trip to Scotland, make sure to play North Berwick.

### Carnoustie Burnside

The often overlooked second course at this golf mecca is a joy to play.

## Panmure

This is where I first fell in love with the courses of the great James Braid. It has a stretch of some of the more unique links holes in the country and maybe the best clubhouse in the world.

## Fortrose & Rosemarkie

An elegantly flowing Braid links set amongst a sea of blinding yellow gorse. Not to be missed on the way to Brora and Golspie.

## Gairloch

A remote seaside nine in the northwest Highlands. Pure fun and always in near-perfect condition. The par-five 8th is one of the best holes in Scotland.

## Hopeman

Worth the visit for the par-three 12th hole alone. If you are there when the whins are blooming, it is a sight you will never forget. A very friendly golf club.

## Machrie Bay

Another nine-hole Arran favorite. The great Walter Hagen played an exhibition match here in 1937, by mistake. Perfect for a round with hickory clubs and worth the price alone just to play the bizarre and wonderful par-four 9th.

## Portmahomack (Tarbat)

A must play when visiting the north. Nine holes on tumbling, links-like farmland. Not far from the wonderful Tain Golf Club.

## Isle of Seil

A short detour off the main road to Oban. Honesty box golf at its finest. Worth a two-hour side trip. Pay your green fee at the corner store/post office.

## Traigh

Nine holes of pure fun. A great wee clubhouse. Brilliant views. All you need in golf.

## Boat of Garten

With apologies to the King's Course at Gleneagles, this is my favorite inland course in Scotland. Simply beautiful, with great hole after great hole. It is, of course, designed by James Braid.

## Lanark

A true inland links designed by Old Tom Morris and James Braid.

## Prestwick St Nicholas

One of the friendliest clubs you could hope to visit, with a wonderful history. The golf is good too. 15-18 is one of the best finishes anywhere.

## Rosehearty

Places like Rosehearty are the reason why golf in Scotland is an almost endless quest of discovery.

## Royal Aberdeen

Historic, ancient and great. After Prestwick, probably my favorite historical links.

## Kilmarnock (Barassie)

Good, solid, Ayrshire links golf with a welcoming staff. A tough, but fun, test.

## Portpatrick

The epitome of headland golf, in the criminally overlooked Dumfries & Galloway region. On a clear day, it rivals the views of any course.

## Stranraer

Braid's last design. So many good holes. He was an elegant designer until the end.

## St. Medan

A nine-hole honesty box mecca on the sea in Dumfries and Galloway.

## Reay

If you are going all the way to Brora, why not drive another 90 minutes to serene Reay? An unchanged, brilliant Braid design. Worth adding a day to your Highlands trip.

## Wick

A traditional Scottish links; the ball runs forever. Don't skip if you are going to Reay.

## Isle of Colonsay

My first introduction to *natural* Scottish golf. Like Iona, you play amongst the sheep on the glorious machair. If you want to experience what playing golf was like in the 1800s, take the ferry to Colonsay. The evening that I spent there with Robbie Wilson in the garden of the Colonsay Hotel is one that I will never forget.

## Brodick

Not a links, but fun, quirky seaside golf. Not to be missed when on Arran.

## Isle of Skye

A stunning nine-hole course on the Sound of Raasay. A lovely walk among an endless variety of colorful native plants. Wonderful.

## Millport

James Braid on top of a small island. Views, blind shots, heather, gorse—it has it all.

## Gullane #3

It is often overlooked by visitors to this East Lothian golf mecca. It should not be.

PUTTING GREEN AND GOAT FELL, BRODICK

# AFTERWORD

BY STEPHEN PROCTOR

I Hartsell, thou Hartsellest, he or she Hartsells, we all Hartsell or are about to Hartsell; and I trust, with apologies to Bernard Darwin, that no traveling golfer needs telling that the verb I am conjugating means to roam Scottish byways in search of the game's living soul the way writer Jim Hartsell does.

In this age when the price of a round at Scotland's premiere links has become an obscenity, and the professional game has been warped beyond recognition by a bottomless pit of money and the ceaseless march of technology, Hartsell's latest book, *A Round of Scottish Courses*, arrives as a declaration of what truly matters in the royal and ancient game.

In his meanderings around his 18 favorite Scottish courses—a list developed over three decades of playing golf over the length and breadth of the nation—Hartsell reminds us of the qualities that caused the Scottish game to become a worldwide addiction in the first place: a lovely walk with friends in a scenic glen, a hole that would make modern architects blush but is an unbridled joy to play, a post-round pint in a wee clubhouse that provides nothing more than cozy comfort, all that is ever truly required.

Hartsell is hardly alone. He is, in truth, the high priest of a growing movement to restore the basic simplicity of golf as a stick-and-ball game that can be enjoyed, as Herbert Warren Wind put it, wherever the sun shines and the grass grows—and not only, as bag-tag hunters would have you believe, at the pricey courses that populate the Top 100 lists.

The signs of this rebellion against how far the game has strayed from its Scottish roots are everywhere—from a growing body of literature extolling authentic and affordable golf experiences to the increasing number of players turning to vintage equipment to restore the lost art of shotmaking.

This yearning to experience golf as it was meant to be played has always been an undercurrent in golf literature, at least since the days when John Stark took American Michael Bamberger to Auchnafree in *To the Linksland* and journalist Tom Morton roared around the Western Isles on his Kawasaki to knock a ball around obscure links like Reay and Stornoway in *Hell's Golfer.*

In recent years, however, no doubt in reaction to skyrocketing prices and the crushing boredom of bomb-and-gouge golf, this quest to reclaim the game's simple pleasures has become a dominant theme, with Hartsell leading the way through his regular contributions to *Links Diary,* his poignant *When Revelation Comes* and now *A Round of Scottish Courses.*

Even before he began writing those two books, Hartsell demonstrated that he was a writer of a different stripe with his *The Secret Home of Golf,* the origin story of an American course with decidedly Scottish vibes, Sweetens Cove Golf Club in South Pittsburg, Tennessee.

Harstell is among a triumvirate of writers extolling the virtues of courses that won't make anyone's Top 100 list. While he was in Scotland, coming to grips with the unspeakable personal tragedy at the heart of *When Revelation Comes,* Robin Down was publishing his tale of golf in the far reaches of the nation in his 2021 book *Golf in the Wild.*

More recently, Richard Pennell has taken up the cause in his column, Pitchmarks, and his 2023 book *Grass Routes,* which revealed his contemplative approach to the game as it took readers to discover such off-the-beaten path English courses as Painswick, Minchinhampton Old and Cleeve Hill. Pennell has since extended wanderings to other parts of the British Isles and added a second volume, *Common Grounds*.

The uprising is by no means limited to literature. On both sides of the Atlantic, an increasing number of players are rejecting modern equipment for vintage clubs, principally persimmons, blades and balata balls, as a consensus seems to have developed among the cognoscenti that golf achieved the ideal balance between talent and technology during the age of Palmer and Nicklaus.

Nor is it simply a question of die-hard retrogrades taking their father's sticks out to the links and posting images of their adventures on social media. High-profile new-media golf outlets like The Fried Egg in the United States and Cookie Jar Golf in the United Kingdom are now sponsoring events restricted to vintage clubs, and they are proving to be wildly popular.

While he has been known to go around his favorite haunts with a few ancient hickories, Hartsell's passion is for authentic golf courses, the regulars who love them unreservedly and the role they play in their communities.

How, then, do we know when we are Hartselling?

We know if we have arrived at the links by ferry. We know if we have paid for our round by stuffing a five pound note in the Honor Box before heading off to the first tee.

We know if the course we are playing has a par of 60-something, features spectacular scenery and is full of wildly creative holes, many of which involve the unmatched thrill of discovering what has become of a blind shot.

We know if the course is lovingly tended by a single greenkeeper who has lived in the neighborhood all his life.

We know if the regulars have been playing golf with one another since they were children—and, especially, if their most fervent hope is that a visitor feels as warmly welcomed as they do and enjoys their links just as much.

Having made pilgrimages to his favorite country in the world for three decades now, Hartsell has found his way to more than a hundred golf courses in every nook and cranny of the kingdom.

From these he has selected the 18 that have taken the firmest grip on his soul—nearly a third of them nine-holers and another third that can only be reached by boat.

Among his choices, only Prestwick, Machrihanish and Cruden Bay are on the lists of bag-tag hunters, but all three share two key qualities that make them fit the broadest definition of Hart-selling.

They possess a landscape as magical as any in Scotland—and it is, after all, the land which makes links golf sublime —and they give visitors that warm sense of being part of the family, the quality, above all others, that has drawn Hartsell to Scotland year after year.

This book is an homage to a slim volume published in 1951 entitled *A Round of Golf Courses*, by English poet and Cambridge Blue Patric Dickinson. It quickly earned a reputation as a classic because, as Bernard Darwin put it in his foreword, Dickinson "can make us feel the particular wind that blows on each individual heath and the flavor of the lunch in each individual clubhouse."

A lovely writer himself, Hartsell is as much a philosopher as a poet. It is not the wind on the heath he captures so much as golf as a birthright and a way of life. Take a wee wander with Hartsell around his favorite Scottish haunts, especially his beloved links of Dunaverty, and even the most jaded modern golfer will find himself reacquainted with the living soul of our game.

**—STEPHEN PROCTOR**
Wittsend Farm
Malabar FL

# ACKNOWLEDGMENTS

"Amicitiae nostrae memoriam spero sempiternam fore"
—Marcus Tullius Cicero, Roman philosopher (60 BCE)

This book is dedicated to two of the nicest men I have ever met, Greg McCrae and David MacBrayne. Over the last five years, during multiple trips to Arran and Kintyre, they have done everything possible to help me with this book. They have invited me, and my family, into their homes. We have become treasured friends.

Stephen Proctor was the first person to read this work. We spent several weeks discussing and editing it extensively. Stephen is a brilliant editor. He never tells you what to write, but knows exactly how to make something better with just a few simple words of advice. I am indebted to him for the unselfish gift of helping me with this book. There is nobody whose opinion on writing that I value more.

I must thank my family for allowing me the time it takes to write a book like this. It encompassed over two years and multiple trips to Scotland. My wife, Jaymaine (or Emma to Donnie MacLean) has made a few of these trips with me and has also fallen in love with my favorite country. Jake and Jonathan are the two best sons I could ever hope to have. They are good people, which means more to me than anything else. My dad, still playing golf at age 81, helped me get started on this journey in 1994. I could not have done it without him. I didn't make enough money for us to even eat and pay rent back then, much less travel to Scotland for golf.

Jamie Darling, Kenny Pallas, Graeme McCubbin, and Stuart Currie, the founders of *The Links Diary*, have been the biggest supporters of my writing for the last six years. They love golf for exactly the same reasons I do. Writing for every one of their 13 wonderful issues has been one of the great joys of my life. I hope to continue for many years to come. More than colleagues, we have become friends. Several of these stories first appeared in *The Links Diary* and have been edited and updated for this book.

Tom Coyne and Travis Hill of *The Golfers Journal* have been wonderful supporters of my writing. I have been fortunate to have a few stories appear in their beautiful, groundbreaking, golf book. The Carradale story first appeared in *The Golfers Journal* and has been updated here.

Jim Sitar, the founder of Back Nine Press, has done more to promote good golf writing and great golf books than anyone that I know of. I am thankful I met Jim by chance at Sweetens Cove in 2018 when I was in the process of writing *The Secret Home of Golf.*

No Laying Up—Todd Schuster, Phil Landes, Chris Solomon, DJ Piehowski, and Neil Schuster—have been supporters of my writing since I first started sending out stories. The genesis of a few of these stories started on their website. The film they produced about *When Revelation Comes* demonstrated a perfect understanding of the book. I hope we can meet again on Arran and at Dunaverty.

These people have also helped me the last few years and supported my writing of this book: William Paterson, Finlay MacDonald, Pam McCrae, Karen Barbour of the Arran History Museum, Tony Burrin, the staff of the Corrie Hotel, Ewan McKinnon, Donnie MacLean, John MacInnes, Chris McBride, Frances Hill, Moyra Paterson, Mairi MacMillan, David Fleming, David Baxter, Simon Barrington, Alasdair MacDougall, Malcolm Murray, Rob Collins, Kevin Moore, Seth Stewart, John Allen, Mark Allen, David Coid, Joshua Ralston, Lam Tong, Chris Hartsell, Charles Hartsell, Wright Thompson, Michael Bamberger, Lorne Rubenstein, Mitch Laurance, Hugh Sinclair, Mark Lee, Robbie Wilson, and James L "Jammy" Erwin of Hewitt-Trussville, Alabama.

# BIBLIOGRAPHY


Atkinson, Tom. *The Lonely Lands: A Guidebook to Argyll* (Barr, Scotland, 1985).

Baillie, Hugh. *Golf at the Back of Beyond: Brora Golf Club, 1891-2000* (Brora, Scotland, 2008).

Bamberger, Michael. *To The Linksland: A Golfing Adventure* (New York, 1992).

Bannantyne, Colin C. *The Shiskine Golf & Tennis Club: A History, 1896-1996* (Blackwaterfoot, Scotland, 1996).

Bauchope, John, Ed.. *The Golfing Annual, 1888-89, Volume 2* (London, 1889).

Boyle, Andrew. *Pictorial History of Arran* (Darvel, Ayrshire, 1994).

Caldwell, David H. *Islay, Jura and Colonsay: A Historical Guide* (Edinburgh, 2001).

Campbell, Thorbjorn. *Arran: A History* (Edinburgh, 2007).

Carmichael, Alasdair. *Kintyre* (London, 1974).

Clougher, T. R., Ed. *Golf Clubs of the Empire, 1930* (London, 1930).

Corcoran, Michael. *Duel in the Sun* (New York, 2002).

Crawford, Robert, Ed. *The Book of Iona* (Edinburgh, 2016).

Crawford, Robin A. *Into the Peatlands* (Edinburgh, 2018).

Darwin, Bernard. *British Golf* (London, 1946).

Darwin, Bernard. *James Braid* (London, 1952).

Darwin, Bernard. *The Darwin Sketchbook* (USA, 1991).

Darwin, Bernard. *The Golf Courses of the British Isles* (London, 1910).

Dickinson, Patric. *A Round of Golf Courses* (London, 1951).

Downie, R. Angus. *All About Arran* (Glasgow, 1933).

Duncan, David Scott. *The Golfing Annual Volume 3, 1889-90.* (London, 1890).

Duncan, David Scott. *The Golfing Annual Volume 5, 1891-92.* (London, 1892).

Drummond, Maldwin. *West Highland Shores* (London, 1990).

Drysdale, Alasdair M. *The Golf House Club, Elie* (Elie, 1975).

Evans A. E. *The Holiday Isle of Arran* (Glasgow, 1933).

Firsoff, V.A. *Arran with Camera & Sketchbook* (London, 1951)

Greig, Andrew. *Preferred Lies: A Journey to the Heart of Scottish Golf* (London, 2006).

Hall, Rev. Charles A. *Isle of Arran* (Edinburgh, 1910)

Hall, Tom S. *Tramping in Arran* (Glasgow, 1927)

Haultain, Arnold. *The Mystery of Golf* (Boston, 1908).

Huber, Jim, *Four Days In July: Tom Watson, the 2009 Open Championship, and a Tournament for the Ages* (New York, 2011).

Hutchinson, Horace. *British Golf Links* (London, 1897).

Johnson, Samuel. *A Journey to the Western Islands of Scotland* (London, 1775).

Kerr, John. *The Golf Book of East Lothian* (Edinburgh, 1896).

Lang, Andrew. *A Short History of Scotland* (Edinburgh, 1911).

Low, John L., Ed. *Nisbet's Golf Yearbook, 1911* (London, 1911).

MacBride, Mackenzie. *Arran of the Bens, the Glens & the Brave* (Edinburgh, 1910).

Macfarlane, Robert. *The Old Ways* (London, 2012).

MacKenzie, Alister. *The Spirit of St. Andrews*
(Chelsea, MI, 1995).

MacMillan, Nigel S.C. *The Campbeltown & Machrihanish Light
Railway* (Newton Abbot, England, 1970).

MacVicar, Angus. *Salt in My Porridge* (London, 1971).

MacVicar, Angus. *Heather In My Ears* (London, 1974).

MacVicar, Angus. *Bees in My Bonnet* (London, 1982).

MacVicar, Angus. *Golf In My Gallowses* (London, 1983).

MacVicar, Angus. *Dunaverty Golf Club: The First Hundred
Years* (Campbeltown, Scotland, 1989).

Martin, Angus. *Kintyre: The Hidden Past* (Kilkerran, Scotland,
1984).

Mathieson, Donald Mackay, Ed. *The Golfer's Handbook*, 1947
(Edinburgh, 1947).

Mathieson, Donald Mackay, Ed. *The Golfer's Handbook*, 1956
(London, 1956).

McKelvie, James A. *Whiting Bay Golf Club, Centenary*
(Arran, Scotland, 1995).

McCarthy, Cormac. *The Road* (New York, 2006).

McDiarmid, D.J. *100 Years of Golf at Machrihanish*
(Campbeltown, Scotland, 1976).

McKinlay, S.L. *Scottish Golf and Golfers: A Collection
of Weekly Columns from the Glasgow Herald,
1956-1980* (Stamford, CT, 1992).

McPhee, John. *The Crofter and the Laird* (New York, 1970).

Moreton, John F. and Ian Cumming. *James Braid and
His Four Hundred Golf Courses* (Worcestershire, 2013).

Morton, Tom. *Hell's Golfer: A Good Walk Spoiled*
(Edinburgh, 1994).

Murphy, Michael. *Golf In The Kingdom* (New York, 1972).

Nalder, Ian. *Scotland's Golf in the Days of Steam: A Selective History of the Impact of the Railways on Golf* (Dalkeith, Scotland, 2000).

Payne, George. *Divine Fury of James Braid* (Edinburgh, 2021).

Pearson, Joan. *Kilmartin: The Stones of History* (Gartocharn, Scotland, date unknown).

Ramsay, Dean. *Reminiscences of Scottish Life and Character* (Edinburgh, 1910).

Ritchie, Graham and Mary Harman. *Argyll and the Western Isles* (Edinburgh, 1985).

Roberts, Ronald J. *A Sense of Place: Kintyre's Remarkable Diaspora* (Campbeltown, 2023).

Rubenstein, Lorne. A *Season in Dornoch: Golf and Life in the Scottish Highlands* (New York, 2003).

Ruskin, John. *The Seven Lamps of Architecture* (London, 1849).

Smail, David Cameron, Ed. *Prestwick Golf Club— Birthplace of the Open* (Prestwick, 1989).

Walker, Sara. *Sara Walker's Highland Fling Cookbook* (New York, 1971).

Ward-Thomas, Pat. *The Long Green Fairway* (London, 1966).

Webb, Sharon. *In the Footsteps of Kings: A Guide to Walks in and Around Kilmartin Glen* (Kilmartin, Scotland, 2012).

Wethered, H.N. and Simpson, Thomas. *The Architectural Side of Golf* (London, 1929).

Wilson III, D.M. and H.R.J. Grant. *Machrihanish: Machaire Shanais, Golf 1880s-1920s* (Worcestershire, 2018).

Wind, Herbert Warren. *Following Through: Herbert Warren Wind On Golf* (New York, 1985).

Withall, Mary. *Easdale, Belnahua, Luing & Seil: The Islands that Roofed the World* (Glasgow, 2001).

Yeadon, David. *Seasons on Harris: A Year in Scotland's Outer Hebrides* (New York, 2006).

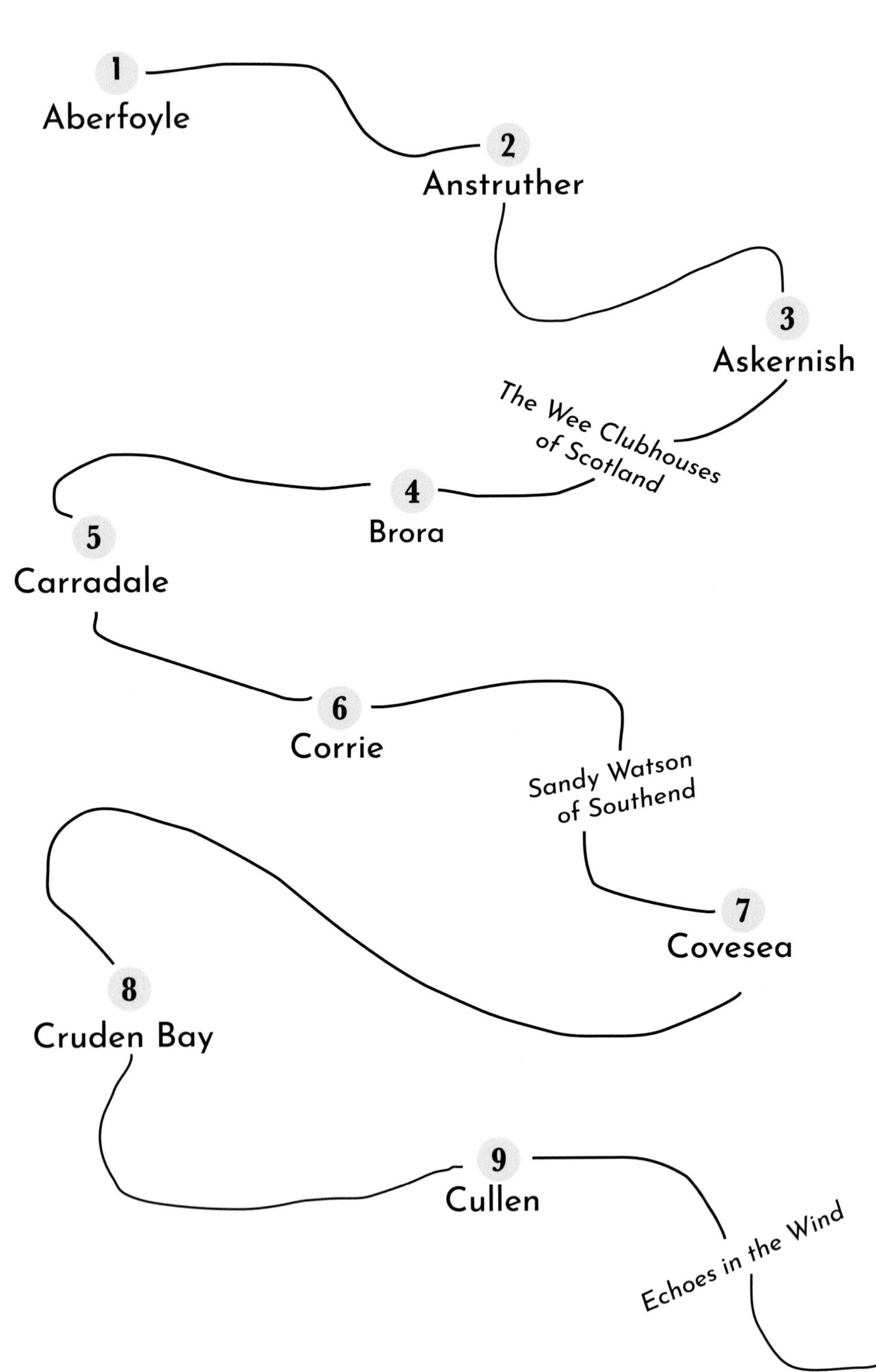

1
Aberfoyle
2
Anstruther
3
Askernish
The Wee Clubhouses of Scotland
4
Brora
5
Carradale
6
Corrie
Sandy Watson of Southend
7
Covesea
8
Cruden Bay
9
Cullen
Echoes in the Wind

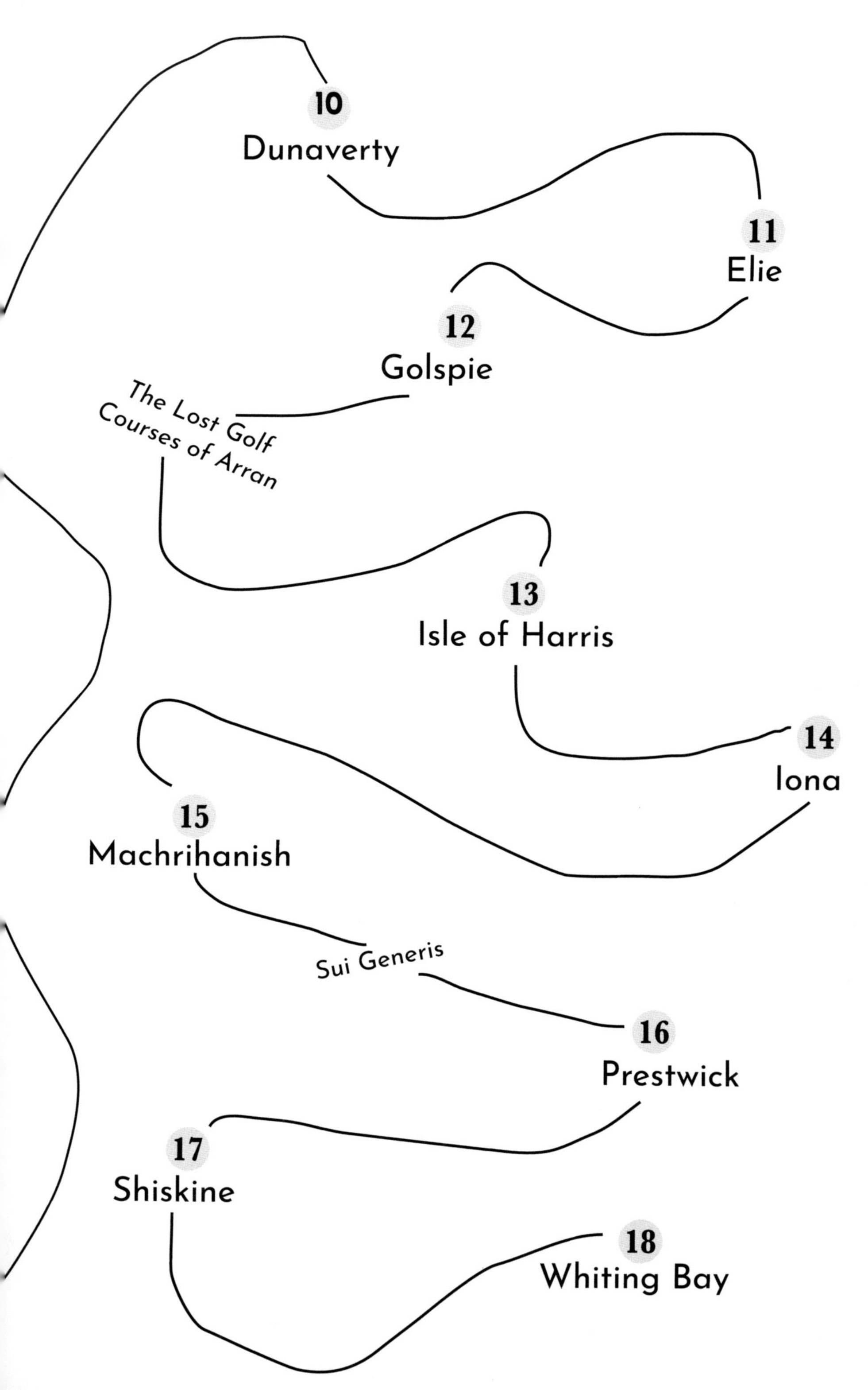

10
Dunaverty
11
Elie
12
Golspie
The Lost Golf
Courses of Arran
13
Isle of Harris
14
Iona
15
Machrihanish
Sui Generis
16
Prestwick
17
Shiskine
18
Whiting Bay